Sanitary Ramblings: Being Sketches and Illustrations of Bethnal Green

Hector Gavin

Nabu Public Domain Reprints:

You are holding a reproduction of an original work published before 1923 that is in the public domain in the United States of America, and possibly other countries. You may freely copy and distribute this work as no entity (individual or corporate) has a copyright on the body of the work. This book may contain prior copyright references, and library stamps (as most of these works were scanned from library copies). These have been scanned and retained as part of the historical artifact.

This book may have occasional imperfections such as missing or blurred pages, poor pictures, errant marks, etc. that were either part of the original artifact, or were introduced by the scanning process. We believe this work is culturally important, and despite the imperfections, have elected to bring it back into print as part of our continuing commitment to the preservation of printed works worldwide. We appreciate your understanding of the imperfections in the preservation process, and hope you enjoy this valuable book.

Just published, 8vo., 9s. cloth,

ON FEIGNED AND FACTITIOUS DISEASES,

Chiefly of Soldiers and Seamen,

ON THE MEANS USED TO SIMULATE OR PRODUCE THEM,

AND N

THE BEST MODES OF DISCOVERING IMPOSTORS.

BEING THE PRIZE ESSAY IN THE CLASS OF MILITARY SURGERY IN THE UNIVERSITY OF EDINBURGH.

BY HECTOR GAVIN, M.D.

FELLOW OF THE ROYAL COLLEGE OF SURGEONS, MD.; F.R.C.S.E.; LECTURER ON FORENSIC MEDICINE AT CHARING-CROSS HOSPITAL; SURGEON TO THE LONDON ORPHAN ASYLUM, AND TO THE BRITISH FEMALE REFUGE, &c. &c.

This Work is intended as a Manual for the Medical Officers of the Army, the Navy, and the Honourable East India Company; and has been published at the desire of the Chiefs of the different Medical Departments of the Public Service, who have long considered a COMPLETE and DISTINCT Work on FEIGNED DISEASES a great desideratum. It is also addressed to the Medical Officers of Gaols, Hospitals, Workhouses, Dispensaries, Benefit Societies, &c., to whom the subject is of great importance. With reference to the first of these, it has met with the approbation of THE HOME SECRETARY and the Inspectors of Prisons, who conceive it will be of great service in these Establishments. It contains a full exposition of the means of distinguishing between the feigned and the real Maniac, and between the Moral Maniac and the Criminal.

SIR JAMES M'GRIGOR, the Director-General of the Medical Department of the Army, considers this Essay a necessary part of the portable library of every Medical Officer, and also recommends every Medical Officer to provide himself with a copy. In this opinion and recommendation SIR WILLIAM BURNETT, the Inspector-General of Naval Hospitals and Fleets, and SIR JOHN WEBB, the Director-General of the Ordnance Medical Department, unite. The Honourable East India Company likewise have considered it necessary to supply a copy to each of their General Hospitals in India.

LONDON: JOHN CHURCHILL, PRINCES STREET, SOHO.

From SIR JAMES M'GRIGOR, BART. MD. F.R.S. and K.C.T.S. *Director-General of the Medical Department of the Army.*

" Dr. Gavin's is the first and only complete work which has appeared on this interesting subject.... I will not fail to promote its circulation among the Medical Officers of the Army by all the means in my power.

" In the opinion of the Director-General of the Medical Department of the Army, Dr. Gavin's work should form part of the portable library of every Medical Officer of the Army.

" I shall take an opportunity of similarly recommending the work to Sir William Burnett, and to Sir John Webb, the Heads of the Navy and Ordnance Medical Departments; and to the Director-General of the Medical Department of he United States Army."

From SIR WILLIAM BURNETT, M.D. K.G.H. *Inspector-General of Naval Hospitals and Fleets.*

" I do hereby certify that I have perused Dr. Gavin's work on Feigned Diseases, &c.; and I am of opinion that a knowledge of its valuable contents would be highly useful to the Public Service."

From SIR JOHN WEBB, M.D. K.G.H. *Director-General of the Ordnance Medical Department.*

" I quite agree with Sir James M'Grigor in the opinion and recommendation of Dr. Gavin's work. I shall do all I can to promote its circulation among the Medical Officers of the Ordnance Department, and shall record my opinion in GENERAL ORDERS."

From DR. HUME, *Physician to the Hon. East India Company.*

" I shall do all I can to promote the circulation of Dr. Gavin's work."

From SIR GEORGE BALLINGALL, M.D. K.G.H. *Professor of Military Surgery in the University of Edinburgh.*

" In this Essay the subject appears to be exhausted.

" My opinion of Dr. Gavin's work has, already, been emphatically expressed, by assigning to it my PRIZE, when it was in a less finished state. I shall have a copy bound up as a prize, which will afford me the best opportunity of making known the favourable opinion which I entertain of his work, and my sense of the labour and intelligence with which he has executed this enlarged edition."

From WILLIAM MORTIMER, M.D. *late Surgeon to the Presidency General Hospital, and Superintendant of the Medical School, Madras.*

"The extent of research so apparent throughout this work is so creditable to Dr. Gavin's industry, and indicative of such a desire to render it, what I consider it to be, the best manual on the subject of which it treats, that I sincerely hope it may meet with the reception it, in my opinion, so well deserves. It is calculated to be of great use both to Military and Naval Surgeons, and I think that every Medical Officer in the Public Service ought to have a copy of it."

"The work ought to be in every practitioner's hands, more especially the Medical Staff of the Army and Navy.... The rules laid down for determining the reality or otherwise of a disease are exceedingly good..... The work may be considered a standard one. We recommend it to such of our readers as desire to become acquainted with the impostures of Malingerers."—*Medico-Chirurgical Review.*

"The general merits of Dr. Gavin's book reflect much credit on his talent and industry. It contains an excellent compilation of all that has been written on the subject, and we can confidently recommend it as a work of reference.—*British and Foreign Medical Review.*

"This work is now the best and most complete monograph on Feigned and Factitious Diseases which we possess, and bids fair to supersede all other works on the same subject.... The author has evidently taken up the subject *con amore*, and the work throughout bears abundant evidence of his zeal, industry, and laborious research in the task he has undertaken. Independent of its professional value, the volume is exceedingly entertaining, inasmuch as it contains numerous curious cases illustrative of the ingenious tricks and devices put in practice by Malingerers. The chapters which treat of Feigned Madness and Moral Insanity are particularly interesting, especially with reference to the opinions recently pronounced in a Court of Law on these important subjects. We can recommend them to the attention of our readers, as containing many useful and instructive hints for the purpose of guiding medical witnesses when called upon to deliver an opinion on suspicious cases before a legal tribunal."—*Provincial Medical Journal.*

"No complete work, before the appearance of Dr. Gavin's, existed upon this subject in our language. To the information on the topic which was common property, the author has added much derived from his own opportunities. Sir James M'Grigor, we understand, highly desired the production of such a work, *candidates for the service being examined upon it*, and recommends every Medical Officer of the army to provide himself with a copy, as a necessary part of his portable library."—*Lancet.*

"The work indicates very extensive research on the part of the a thor.... We can recommend Dr. Gavin's Essay as one which contains much useful information, and as a valuable text-book for those who are engaged in the Military and Naval Services."—*Lancet.*

"The inducement held out by Sir George Ballingall, and the encouragement afforded by Sir James M'Grigor, sufficiently justify the appearance of the present work; but, unquestionably, its own merits would soon have gained it the reputation which it deserves, even had it not been heralded by the praise of influential men.... We can conscientiously commend the work. The diligence with which authorities have been sought out, and information amassed, deserves the highest praise. The work, in fact, is, we believe, the best digest of information on the subject of which it treats."—*London and Edinburgh Monthly Journal of Medical Science.*

"It must be apparent that the work is one of great importance to that part of the medical profession which is connected with the Army or the Navy. Combined with extensive experience, this volume displays a vast range of reading, ancient and modern, on the part of the author. The accumulation of facts and cases is surprising from its variety and number. Many of the instances adduced are so extraordinary in their nature, that they would have been deemed wholly incredible, unless supported by testimony not to be impeached."—*Naval and Military Gazette.*

"Dr. Gavin's treatise may be considered as a most acceptable addition to the library of such Medical Assistants as seek occupation in the Public Service. The various diseases simulated and produced, are minutely, accurately, and clearly discussed, and the suitable methods of detection explained. To the valuable information already developed in monographs, our author has superadded important practical precepts, and much novel matter from the treatises of Continental Surgery, little known in these countries.

"Dr. Gavin's laborious and very useful compilation should be in the hands of the Medical Officer of every department of the Public Service."—*Dublin Medical Press.*

"Dr. Gavin's Essay is a very creditable performance; it richly deserves to reach a second edition."—*London Medical Gazette.*

"This volume opens a curious and interesting chapter in the history of human nature—a chapter studied but by a few, and scarcely even apprehended by the mass of observers.... Among the many diseases which may be feigned for fraudulent purposes, MADNESS has recently been brought into peculiar notice, through an epidemic apprehension, that the facility of deception will tempt to the perpetrating great crimes against society. On this point Dr. Gavin affords some curious information.... The spirit which pervades Dr. Gavin's volume is that of an enlightened and humane philosophy."—*Athenæum.*

"Dr. Gavin has given an excellent digest of the opinions and statements already recorded on this interesting subject, and has added many instructive original cases to those which he already possessed. At the present period, Dr. Gavin's work will be of peculiar interest to those who are desirous of possessing an account of the views taken by the most eminent of the profession on the subject of MORAL INSANITY.... For a very excellent account of the whole of this curious subject we must refer to the author.—*Gateshead Observer.*

a
w
ti
n
a
p
si
S

o
b
a
c
a
in
M

lil
v
di
fo
a
S

th
P

re

n
m
d
th
th
so
th

al
or
D
se
th
w

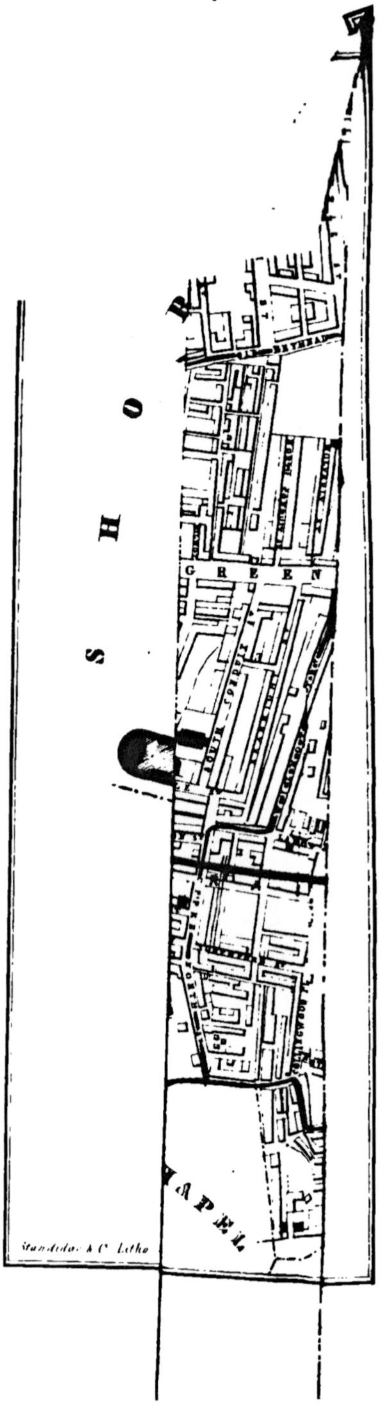

SANITARY RAMBLINGS.

BEING

SKETCHES AND ILLUSTRATIONS,

OF BETHNAL GREEN.

A TYPE

OF THE CONDITION OF THE METROPOLIS

AND OTHER LARGE TOWNS.

BY

HECTOR GAVIN, M.D. F.R.C.S.E.

MEMBER OF THE COMMITTEES OF THE
HEALTH OF TOWNS AND OF LONDON ASSOCIATIONS,
LECTURER ON FORENSIC MEDICINE, AND PUBLIC HEALTH,
CHARING-CROSS HOSPITAL.
&c., &c.

LONDON:

JOHN CHURCHILL, PRINCES STREET, SOHO.

1848.

PRINTED AT THE HEALTH OF TOWNS PRINTING OFFICE,
107, ST. MARTIN'S LANE.

" I believe that the highest attainable salubrity may be secured to cities and towns, by attention to matters that, with us, have been very much neglected; that by a proper construction of habitations, a proper ventilation, sewerage, supply of water, and the daily removal of refuse of every kind by scavengers, a town population may become quite as healthy as that of the country.—*Martin. Second Report, Health of Towns Commission*, p. 118.

I turned into an alley 'neath the wall—
And stepped from earth to hell.—The light of Heaven,
The common air was narrow, gross, and dim—
The tiles did drop from the eaves; the unhinged doors
Tottered o'er inky pools, where reeked and curdled
The offal of a life; the gaunt-haunched swine
Growled at their christened playmates o'er the scraps.
Shrill mothers cursed; wan children wailed; sharp coughs
Rang through the crazy chambers; hungry eyes
Glared dumb reproach, and old perplexity,
Too stale for words; o'er still and webless rooms,
The listless craftsmen through their elf-locks scowled.

THE SAINT'S TRADEGY.—KINGSLEY.

TO THE MOST NOBLE

THE MARQUIS OF NORMANBY,

PRESIDENT OF THE HEALTH OF TOWNS' ASSOCIATION.

My Lord,

No one has a higher claim to the regard of all those who have enrolled themselves under the banner of Sanitary Reform than your Lordship. Whether as President of the 'Health of Towns' Association," or as a Peer of the Realm, your Lordship has ever, in the proper place, and at the proper time, manifested the most anxious desire to provide for the physical welfare (and with the physical welfare, the moral and social amelioration) of your countrymen. Early in the field, earnest in the cause, constant in your efforts, and ready to battle prejudice and ignorance, is the history of your career. While the band of Sanitary Reformers was like but a hand's breadth in the horizon, then were you their chief; and when, now, they are numbered by their hundreds, and their thousands, and when the feeling of the country has responded to your enlightened and benevolent designs, it becomes all who have fought under your standard, and numbered themselves your followers, to testify their respect to you, my Lord, who have so constantly, and so ably, advocated their cause. It is with such feelings that I beg to dedicate to your Lordship the following pages, in the hope that that result will follow which would be most acceptable to you; namely, the arousing in the minds of local authorities and of the gentry the desire to afford to the working population " the modest comforts of an English home," and that " sound condition of body and mind, without which no luxury can be enjoyed, and with which there is hardly any privation that may not be endured."

I have the honour to be,
My Lord,
Your Lordship's most obedient servant,
HECTOR GAVIN.

January, 1848.

REPORT, &c.

In undertaking to draw up a Report on the present sanitary condition of the parish of Bethnal-green, I was actuated by the conviction that I should find in operation in that parish all those leading elements which tend to deteriorate the health, and prematurely to destroy no inconsiderable proportion of the population of large towns. I was also actuated by the conviction that it was impossible to account for the profound indifference which prevails amongst a great part of the people generally, and which is undoubtedly participated in by the authorities of this populous parish, itself constituting no mean town, with regard to the existence of the agents which injure health, and destroy life, but by believing that they were ignorant as to the amount and extent of the ills which they endured. To believe that the middle and upper classes were fully cognisant that multitudes of their fellow-beings have their health injured, their lives sacrificed, their property squandered, their morals depraved, and the efforts to christianise them set at nought by the existence of certain well-defined agents, and yet to find them either making no effort to alleviate, or to remove these misfortunes, or with a stern heart denying their existence, would be to charge these classes with the most atrocious depravity, and the most cruel heartlessness and selfish abandonment. It is impossible to suppose that love and charity are so utterly unknown to this great Metropolis, celebrated beyond all other cities for the magnificence of its public charities and the vastness of its benevolent contributions. I have, then, but to lay bare the naked truth, as to the state of one part of this vast city; and I believe that the hearts of many will be warmed and their spirits aroused to assist those who have undertaken the great work of sanitary improvement and social amelioration.

I am strengthened in the conviction which I entertain, and which I have thus put forth, by the opinions of men who have dedicated abilities of no common order to the elucidation of the bearings of the sanitary question on the poor and on the rich. "I have universally observed in this district," says Dr. Reid, "*that a thorough and distinct exposition of the realities of that amount of discomfort, disease, and death, that are justly attributable to causes that may be easily reduced in virulence, will lead numbers to assist in the amelioration of the condition of the poor*, as they become more sensibly alive to the great benefits that arise from a little timely assistance or interference, and to the magnitude of those evils that oppress so many of our fellow-creatures, and to which millions are habitually exposed, without that consciousness of their existence which is essential for the development and prosecution of active measures of relief."

"Owing to the vastness of London," says Mr. Martin,—" owing to the moral gulf which there separates the various classes of its inhabitants—its several quarters may be designated as assemblages of towns rather than as one city; and so it is in a social sense, and on a smaller scale, in other towns; *the rich know nothing of the poor;* the mass of misery that festers beneath the affluence of London and of the great towns is not known to their wealthy occupants. This arises not from want of kindly feeling or charity towards the poor; far from it, but from the absence of such institutions as should call the attention of the higher and of the wealthy classes to this subject."

It is true, that some partial attempts have been made to display, both locally and generally, many of the remediable ills which the inhabitants of London endure; but no complete elucidation of the sanitary state of any one district has as yet been prominently brought forward for the purpose of securing the sympathy of the public. This attempt I have made in the following pages. I have greatly to regret that the difficulties thrown in my way in my endeavours to procure information have been very considerable. Nevertheless, I believe that the exposition which is made will be quite sufficient to secure for me the great end at which I aim, namely, on the part of the public, and of individuals, a more extended acquaintance with the state in which many thousands of their fellow-beings exist; a more correct knowledge of the causes which produce the mortality, pauperism, immorality, and crime which are the lot of so many of those born in suffering poverty; and a more profound conviction not only of the facility of removing many of the deteriorating and destructive influences, but of the absolute necessity of actively and energetically setting about the work of their suppression.

I cannot but believe that when the rich and affluent who reside in the parish of Bethnal Green, and there are some both rich and affluent, and when the authorities become acquainted with the true bearings of the evils produced by the neglect of sanitary measures, they will at least avail themselves of the means which are at present within their power, to cleanse and purify the foul streets and filthy dwellings of their miserable fellow-parishioners.

I am firmly convinced that were they only to cleanse their streets, remove the dust and garbage-heaps from the houses and dwellings of the poor, and cleanse, or cause to be cleansed, the filthy cesspools and privies which everywhere pollute the surface of this dirty parish; nay, were they only effectually to put into operation Lord Morpeth's Act for the suppression of nuisances, they would effect an amount of good of which they have no conception; they would obtain the approbation of every right-thinking inhabitant, and the blessing of thousands of the neglected and suffering, yet patient, poor.

I beg to return my best thanks to the Registrar-General for his great politeness and attention in affording me every facility for acquiring an exact knowledge of the mortality of the parish. I have also to return my warmest thanks to the parochial medical officers, who, with the generous sympathy so continually manifested by the members of their liberal but ill-remunerated profession, gave me their valuable aid, day after day, in prosecuting my inquiries. I trust that the exposition of their labours, contained in this Report, may not be without its effect in obtaining for them a more liberal remuneration for their services.

The parish of Bethnal Green has long possessed an unenviable notoriety on account of its neglected state and defective sanitary condition. It forms one or the eastern districts of the Metropolis—districts which are the most unhealthy of all comprised in the Metropolitan Registration Returns. They invariably suffer much more than the other metropolitan districts from epidemics and unusual causes of mortality.

Thus, if we take the mortality above the average of the last five autumns, corrected for the increase of the population, during the week ending Nov. 27: arising from influenza, we shall find—

That while the increase in the mortality of the west districts was 22·6 per cent.

In the south districts it was ....41·6 —
In the north districts .... 45.1 —
In the central districts .... 62·2 —
In the east districts .... 102·9 —

In the east districts of London, therefore, the mortality has been more than doubled by the prevalence of influenza.

Bethnal Green has an area of one square mile and four-ninths, of which at least one-third consists of an open space. It is bounded on the north by the healthy parish of Hackney, and the unhealthy parish of Shoreditch; on the west it is likewise bounded by Shoreditch; on the south it is bounded by the still more unhealthy districts of Spitalfields, Mile-end New Town, Whitechapel, and Mile-end Old Town; on the east, except for about 300 yards, it is bounded by Poplar.

The parish of Bethnal Green is divided into four districts; namely, the Green, the Church, the Town, and the Hackney-road districts. These are likewise the registration districts.

The Green district is by far the largest in extent. It lies to the east of the parish, and is bounded on the north by South Hackney, on the east by Poplar, on the south by Mile-end Old Town, and on the west by the Hackney-road, and the Church districts. By far the greater part of this space is open and uncovered by buildings; it contains the workhouse, and Dr. Warburton's lunatic asylum, Globe Town, and the Cambridge-road. To the north-east is a portion of the Victoria Park. The district may appropriately be termed suburban, as it forms the very outskirt of London in the eastern direction. There are two cemeteries in this district,—the North-east London Cemetery, in the hands of a private gentleman, and the Victoria Park Cemetery, possessed by a company.

The Church district is only about one-fourth or one-fifth the size of the Green district. It is bounded on the north by the Hackney-road district, on the east by the Green district, on the south by Whitechapel and the Town district, and on the east by the Town district. With the exception of the open spaces, on either side of the railway, formed by the erasement of numerous houses and some streets, there are no wide open spaces. The houses cannot, however, be said to be densely crowded together. It contains no public buildings (except churches). This district contains two large grave-yards, possessed by the Jews.

The Town District is still smaller than the Church district. It lies between the Hackney-road and Church districts on the north, and the last-mentioned district on the east; Spitalfields and Mile-end New Town on the south; and part of the Hackney-road district and Shoreditch on the west. The whole of this district may be said to be closely built on, and densely crowded, presenting the very opposite characters to the Green district. There are no open spaces whatever in this district.

The Hackney-road district is about the same size as the Church district. It is bounded on the north by Shoreditch and South Hackney; on the east by the Green district; on the south by the Town and Church districts; and on the west by Shoreditch. This district may be subdivided into two—the Hackney-road district proper, which constitutes the fifth medical relief district, and that portion which adjoins, and really forms part of the Town district. The Hackney-road district proper is chiefly composed of a better class of buildings: the other is characterised by everything that can disgrace a town.

The parish is likewise divided by the guardians of the poor into five medical relief districts. As this division is a much more perfect one, in a sanitary point of view, than the poor-rate and registration division, I shall adopt it in giving an account of the parish.

The first of the medical relief districts contains the Green distrct.

The second consists of the greater part of the Church district.

The third consists of the greater part of the Town district and a small part of the Church district.

The fourth, which is bounded on the east by Shoreditch, consists of the worst part of the Hackney-road division, and a part of the Town district.

The fifth consists of the Hackney-road district, with the exception of the worst part, which has been transferred to No. 4 division.

DISTRICT I.

This district is remarkable, as being the eastern outskirt of London, nearly as far it extends from north to south. To the north, as to the east, this district is perfectly free. The north-eastern portion contains a small part of the Victoria Park—a park which Lord Morpeth, with the most earnest desire to advance the physical welfare of the inhabitants of the dense localities in its vicinity, has rendered extremely attractive, and in which he has provided the requisites for various gymnastic exercises. An artificial water is likewise being formed, at his desire, for the purpose of affording to the weary and soiled artisan the refreshment of bathing. In this district there has likewise, in connection with the Victoria Park, and through the Woods and Forests, been lately laid down nearly half a mile of main sewer, which will serve effectually to drain the ground, which has been prepared for building on, west of the park. Besides this free space, this district contains large open pieces of ground within itself; namely, Bethnal Green, and the extensive piece of ground south of it, reaching to the railway, which has recently been provided by Dr. Warburton for the use of the lunatics in his establishment. The houses are scattered, and there is abundance of space. We are not therefore to look for those diseases which are peculiar to over-crowded districts. There are, however, two elements of a high mortality in the returns for this district; first, the workhouse, which shall be considered separately; and next, Dr. Warburton's lunatic asylum, which will follow it. The houses in the direction of Old Ford are remarkable for their great deficiency of drainage and for their dirty streets, but there are, comparatively, few courts, and still fewer alleys; where they do exist, however, they are in no respect superior to the filthy hovels and wretched abodes common to the third, fourth, and fifth districts. The gradual conversion of summer-houses, cabins, and wooden-sheds into human habitations is to be remarked, in its elementary stage, in Whisker's-gardens.

The contrast between the condition of the common and Macadamized roads in most parts of this district, and those in Cambridge-road and Palestine-place, may be considered as the extreme. In the former there is scarcely any drainage or sewerage; in the latter they are both excellent. The former are always very dirty, sometimes abominably filthy; the latter are always clean.

The following are the details of my investigations into the condition of this district, and the result of my personal inspections;—

CAMBRIDGE-ROAD, 1, may be said to extend from Hackney-turnpike to Mile-end-gate. This includes Bethnal-green and the Dog-row. This road from Hackney is kept clean; it continues clean till it approaches towards Mile-end-gate, where it becomes extremely dirty, and where refuse and garbage are frequently to be found on its surface. The gutters here become full, and mud-heaps are to be found every few yards; the footpath has been well paved. Notwithstanding the great traffic on this road, and the great importance of efficient sewerage, there is no sewer from the north side of Bethnal-green to Three Colt-lane, and the greater part of the Dog-row is likewise without a sewer. The difference of the cleanliness of the branch streets, where there is efficient sewerage, from the filthiness where there is none, or inefficient sewerage, is most marked. On the west side of Cambridge-road, north of Bethnal-green, there is a very dirty yard, where dung-heaps abound, and pig-styes omit offensive effluvia.

GEORGE-ST., O. B. G. R., 2.—The gutters here are loaded with fœtid filth, which accumulates from the surface-drains of the houses. This filth passes by an open ditch into the neighbouring brick-field, first receiving the contents of a small ditch which runs at the back of the houses.

PEACOCK-ALLEY, 3.—This is a cluster of miserable houses; the gutter fronting them is full of most fœtid, muddy filth; dust, and garbage-heaps are common. Two stand-pipes supply eleven houses with water, but there is no receptacle to receive, and preserve it; the want of such a receptable is grievously complained of. 3s. 3d. are the rent of each house, consisting of two rooms, one on the ground floor (which is very damp), and a garret.

PARADISE-ROW, 4.—This row of houses fronts Bethnal-green; at the north end, it is an alley. These houses present all the external characters of decency and comfort; nevertheless, the following fact will explain how much the health of the inhabitants is dependent on external circumstances:—A gentleman, named

Knight, rashly, and in ignorance of the locality, purchased the lease of No. 1, which forms the eastern end of Bethnal-green-road. Immediately after taking up his residence there he became ill, and, shortly after, died of typhus, in an aggravated form. On inspection of the neighbouring premises, I discovered "Paradise Dairy" immediately behind his house. In this dairy sixteen cows and twenty swine are usually kept. The animal remains and decomposing vegetable refuse were piled up a considerable height above a hollow adapted to receive them. This conservation of the refuse takes place in order that a sufficiently large quantity may accumulate. Moreover, the soakage from the neighbouring privies found its way into this receptacle for manure and filth. The surface of the yard was dirty and covered with refuse. Even in the street, the offensiveness of this nuisance was obviously apparent to every passer-by. The occupiers of this dairy nevertheless asserted the place to be perfectly clean and wholesome.

MOCKFORD BUILDINGS, 5.—This is a blind court or alley containing five houses. The houses are two-roomed, and let for 3s. a week. In one room seven persons slept, and six now sleep; the seventh died of pneumonia. The four children of the parties who reside in this wretchedly damp place have all been ill with low fever. The room in which they sleep is 9 feet by 7 in width and 7½ feet high.

SUFFOLK-ST., &c, 6.—The roadway of this street is in the most deplorably filthy condition; north of the railway it is a perfect quagmire. Garbage and refuse of all sorts are deposited by the side of the wall. By the side of the arch, No. 100, is a low yard, from which the most offensive smells arise. The place is excessively filthy, and abominably dirty.

BARNSLEY-ALLEY, 7.—There is an open space in front of this alley, covered with garbage.

NEW SOMRFORD-ST., 8.—The road is broken up, and excessively dirty.

NORFOLK-ST., CAMBRIDGE-ROAD, 9.—This street is in a very dirty condition, with mud-heaps scattered over it every yard or two.

CROSS-ST., CAMBRIDGE-ROAD, 10.—This street is similarly covered with mud-heaps.

NORTHAMPTON-ST., CAMBRIDG-ROAD, 11.—This street likewise is covered with mud-heaps. There is a cow-yard in it.

DARLING-ROW, CAMBRIDGE-ROAD, 12.—Similar mud-heaps encumber this street.

ESSEX-ST., NOTHAMPTON-ST., 13.—Mud-heaps and scattered garbage, and collections of dung and refuse encumber this street.

JOHN-ST., 14.—On entering one of the houses in this dirty street I found four persons sleeping in a room six feet high, and seven feet by eight in width. Nearly the whole space was taken up with the bed and a few articles of furniture.

JOHN'S COURT, JOHN-ST., 15.—There is but one stand tap to the four houses, which are very damp. They are two-roomed, and the rent is 2s. 6d. a week.

GARDEN-PLACE, JAMES-ST., 16.—Is entered by a [narrow alley, three or four houses are stuck on the damp clay, with small yards in front, on which every kind of refuse is thrown. No dust heaps are accumulated, but the refuse is left to lie where it is thrown. Fever has been very prevalent in this place, in one house nearly every inmate has been attacked. In the alley leading to these horrid and neglected spots is a large pig-stye; it is close to the houses, and emits the most disgusting and sickening odours. I could not remain to make notes of this place, so overpowering was the abominable stench.

JAMES-ST., 17.—In this street there is a very large yard, in which stores of waste tin, zinc, &c., are preserved and sorted. Although the place cannot be termed an offensive nuisance, nevertheless the gradual accumulation of refuse, which necessarily takes places, causes the surface of the ground in wet weather to emit unwholesome effluvia. There is likewise in this street, a small yard for the collection of ashes, and dust, and dirt of various kinds. These are preserved and sorted. There is also in this yard garbage and manure-heaps. At the end of the street there is another tin yard, not quite so large as the one just mentioned. This street though very dirty, and with the gutters full of offensive black slime and mud, is not now in the impassable state described by Dr. Southwood Smith nine years and a-half ago. This I attribute to an excellent sewer which passes from the south-east of Bethnal-green, the whole length of Green-street. Neither do I find there the nightman's-yard which he describes, and which I therefore presume, has been done away with.

ELY-PLACE, DIGBY-PLACE, 18.—This place is in a most dilapidated state; most of the houses are in a wretched condition. Two of the houses are considerably below the level of the alley. Even now, on a dry frosty day, the soil in front of them is very wet, but after rains the hollow becomes a swamp. Much sickness and disease always prevail here. In one room I found five persons residing, two were ill with fever.

DIGBY-ST., GLOBE-ROAD. 19.—In this *most dirty street*, exists one of the most atrocious nuisances which it is possible to create. One cannot conceive the toleration of such an abomination by the law, without being overwhelmed with amazement and regret, I would almost say, despondency. A person named Baker, lately dead, here formed a receptable for every kind of manure. The premises have a frontage of 450 feet, and are about 140 feet in depth. With the exception of a small space in front, and on either side, the whole of the area is filled with every variety of manure in every stage of offensive and disgusting decomposition; the manure is piled up to a considerable height, and is left to dry in the sun; but, besides this table mountain of manure, extensive and deep lakes of putrefying *night soil* are dammed up with the more solid dung, and refuse, forming together, mountain and lake, a scene of the most disgusting character; degrading alike to its late possessor and to the authorities who permit its existence. If foul privies, and overflowing cesspools are justly considered sources of disease and death,—if they are correctly termed insidious and fatal poisons,—if it be impossible as is stated by the Government Commissioners, that any people can be healthy who live on a soil permeated by cesspools—in what light must we consider this wholesale manufactory of a poison, at once most disgusting and most deadly, and how shall we regard those who supinely and apathetically submit their own fellow-beings to its lethal operation. The decomposing organic particles which are ever being set free from this putrescent mass, are wafted by each wind that blows, over a population to whom they bring disease and death, as surely as, though more insidiously than, the deadly simoom.

DIGBY WALK, GLOBE ROAD, 19.—In fit character with the distressing and degrading scene last visited, is this alley, which is in a state of the most beastly dirt. More than half of this horrid alley is covered with a stagnant pool of most offensive and filthy slime, and mud, in some places, to the depth of a foot. Some of the houses, which abut on it, are unfinished, but the yards of the older houses present a character little dissimilar to the stagnant gutter, or ditch itself. The refuse from a pig-stye drains into this gutter, and adds pungency to its offensiveness. This place is private property, and the landlord of the new houses has built a cesspool, into which to drain his houses, but he will not permit the other houses in the alley to drain into this cesspool, unless the parish pay to him 1l., a sum which it will not pay. Verily, one case of typhus would cost much more than the small sum asked to keep this place clean.

BAKER-STREET, GREEN-STREET, 20.—One of the yards in this street is in a filthy state, and contains a heap of manure.

KNOTTISFORD-STREET, 21.—At the end of this street there is a cow-yard; pigs are likewise kept here. The place sends off most offensive smells.

CHARLES-STREET, 22.—Garbage and refuse are freely distributed on the surface of this dirty street.

CEMETERY-PLACE, 23.—Consists of a few wretched houses, near the Victoria Park Cemetery.

WEST-STREET, GREEN-STREET, 24.—This street is *most filthy*. Many of the houses on the south side are below the level of the road, and are consequently very damp.

VIOLET-ROW, 25.—This is an excessively dirty place. In front of the houses, in this row, there is a small space which is covered with muddy and slimy pools, with garbage, and with refuse heaps.

HARROLD-STREET, GREEN-STREET, 26.—In No. 10 in this street I found eight persons, who live and sleep in one room. The room is 10 feet by 6 feet, and 9 feet high. The bed and furniture filled no inconsiderable portion of the room; the children had low fever. The house contains two rooms on the ground floor, and a work-room above; another family occupied the other room. For the one room, and the use of part of the work-room, 2s. 9d. a week are paid. At the corner of this place is a large open brick field.

TYPE-STREET, GREEN-STREET, 27.—This street must have been intended as a type of the rest of the district which I had to visit. It was in *the most filthy state possible*, the stagnant pools of fœtid, and putrid mud with their green scum, presented an aspect as offensive to the sight, as the smell was repulsive:

pig-styes and dung-heaps heightened the foulness of the effluvia, and rendered the place horrible. Towards the end of this street is an opening for the commencement of a new street. A pool of fœtid slime, twenty-three yards long, fills up part of the opening. A gutter, cut in the roadway, conducts the slimy refuse from the filthy street into this pond; two small gutters likewise lead into it from separate houses.

SYDNEY-STREET, GREEN-STREET, 28.—The same kind of thickened, black, slimy, and putrescent mud, with the green scum of vegetable life sprouting on its surface, fills the gutters and hollows of this street; a pig-stye abutting on it increases the sum of nuisances.

CROSS-STREET, GREEN-STREET, 29.—*This street is utterly beastly*, the gutters are filled with the same kind of offensive putrifying mud. But

PLEASANT-PLACE, 30, presents the *ne plus ultra* of street abomination. It is impossible to conceive how utterly filthy and abominable this street is; to be estimated it must be seen. The broken up road is filled in its hollows, and covered on its surface, so as to be nearly impassable (even this dry frosty day) with the putrescent muddy slime already referred to; and this is its state shortly after it has been cleansed, as it is absurdly termed, by the parish authorities. The street is nothing more or less than an elongated lake or canal; only, in place of water, we have a black, slimy, muddy compost of clay and putrescent animal and vegetable remains. Fever has visited this spot, and in one house has been very fatal.

KING-STREET, OLD FORD-LANE, 31.—This street is little, if at all, better than the preceding, and the same discreditable observations apply to it. It is quite evident that such a condition of things, as is above referred to, must be destructive of all personal cleanliness and comfort, subversive of moral energy, and dangerous to health.

OLD FORD-LANE, 32.—By the side of this lane there runs a black ditch.

BONNER'S-LANE, 33.—There is also by the side of this narrow lane, and fronting the houses, a black gutter, which may almost be termed a ditch. As there is no drainage whatever to this place, whenever a shower of rain falls, the contents of this gutter are washed over, and cover, the pathway. At the present time it smells very offensive. Fever is generally very prevalent here.

WHISKER'S GARDENS, 34.—This is a very extensive piece of ground, which is laid out, in neat plots, as gardens. The choicest flowers are frequently raised here, and great taste, and considerable refinement are evidently possessed by those who cultivate them. Now, among the cultivators are the poor—even the very poor—of Bethnal Green, for the few gentlemen who likewise have their gardens here are inconsiderable in number. I am confirmed, by the neatness and taste displayed in these gardens, in the justness of according to the poor a much higher sense of social comfort, and of the refinements of life, than is usually granted to them. The weary artisan and the toil-worn weaver here dedicate their spare hours, in the proper seasons, to what has always been considered a refined, as well as an innocent recreation, the cultivation of beautiful flowers. The love of the beautiful, and the sense of order which are readily accorded to the artisan, or weaver, in his neat garden, surrounded by the choicest dahlias or tulips carefully cultivated, are denied to him when visited in his filthy, dirty street. When seen in his damp and dirty home, he is generally accused of personal uncleanliness, and a disregard of the commonest appearances of decency and regularity; yet, in his garden, he displays evidences of a refined taste and a natural love of beauty and of order. The two are irreconcileable, and as the one sentiment is natural and spontaneous, we are irresistibly led to regard the personal uncleanness of the poor, and the impurities which surround their houses, as the results of agencies foreign to the individual. Attached to all these little plots of ground are summer-houses. In the generality of cases, they are mere wooden sheds, cabins, or huts; but a few are more solid erections. It is very greatly to be regretted that the proprietors of these gardens should permit the slight and fragile sheds in them to be converted into abodes for human beings. It is impossible to view the change of these summer-houses into permanent dwellings but as the commencement of the lamentable state of things which at present exists in George-gardens, and Gale's-gardens, and, in its worst forms, in Greengate and Weatherhead-gardens; places which are yet to be described. Of the hundreds of summer-houses in Whisker's-gardens, some sixteen or twenty only have as yet been converted into human habitations; but the following facts regarding them sufficiently point out the deplorable consequences of the change. The "houses" in these gardens are partly wooden, partly brick sheds, altogether unadapted to any other purpose than the most temporary protection from the inclemency of the weather. Sometimes they are divided into rooms; they are planted on the damp, undrained ground. The privies are sheds, erected over holes in the ground; the soil, itself, is removed from these holes, and is dug into the ground to promote its fertility; thus carrying out an apparently scientific design to poison by fever the inmates of the neighbouring dwellings. The supply of water is derived from wells sunk in the ground, thus manured; sometimes one well supplies one, sometimes two dwellings. Holes are likewise dug in the ground into which to throw the foul water. I have been thus particular in my description of these gardens, as the description will serve to explain the existence of such places as George-gardens down to the infamous Weatherhead-gardens, now become the abodes of the scum of society. Two cases of typhus occurred to the parochial medical officer in these gardens, one presenting a malignant character which died.

PARK-STREET, 35.—This street is covered with mud-heaps, garbage, and refuse, and is very dirty.

NORTH-PLACE, GREEN-STREET, 36.—This street is likewise covered with refuse, dung, and garbage. Pig-styes add to the filthiness of the place and the foulness of the effluvia. Hooping-cough and measles abound here.

BERNHAM-SQU., 37.—This square consists of scattered buildings in gardens, and forms a remarkable exception to the foulness of the places last visited, in being *tolerably clean*.

Grosvenor-place, Globe-street, 38.—In this street the black slimy filth has been cleansed out from the gutters, and carefully spread over the surface of the road, which is broken up, and in a most beastly condition, covered with decaying refuse and garbage. At the end of it is a pig-stye, and a stable.

Providence-place, Blue Anchor-lane, 39.—In front of this place is a space where every kind of refuse and filth is swept, and where the water stagnates and causes the more rapid decomposition of the garbage.

Prussia or Blue Anchor-lane, 40.—This lane is nearly in an impassable state for carts; it is quite broken up, and is most filthy. There is a cow-yard in it, with seven or eight dung-heaps. Twenty-two houses have been recently built, but the roadway before them is passable.

Martha-court, Martha-street, 41.—A wretched court leading out of Martha-street. There are thirteen houses in it, in a most dilapidated condition; they are two-roomed, and are very damp, as is shown by the walls. One tap with a cock serves to supply the whole thirteen houses; but there are three privies in an offensive state. There is one dust corner. 3s. and 2s. 6d. a week are the rents of these houses.

Chester-street, 42, also termed Behind Chester-place.—This short street is in a most lamentable state, from the want of efficient drainage, a state which is the more discreditable, as the main sewer passes along Chester-place for 156 feet. The gutter is flooded with filth and slimy mud; the gutter gradually widens out till the whole breadth of this street, eight yards, is covered with stagnant water and fœtid mud; but not only does it cover the whole roadway, but it also extends some distance down a roadway at right angles to it (improperly termed Chester-place). The gutter is deepened at the extremity of the street, and into it a house drain pours its supply of fluid refuse. Between this gutter, and the stagnant pool all kinds of vegetable refuse are profusely scattered, and are gradually passing into decomposition—garbage, dung, potato-peelings, cabbage-leaves, sloes, and dust and dirt of all descriptions.

Helen's-place, Chester-place, 43.—In this place there is a large tin-yard, similar to that referred to in James-street. Fronting a narrow footpath is a filthy black ditch, 45 feet long. On the other side are three very small yards; these are connected with four *houses*. These houses, better termed sheds, consist of one room; they are barely seven feet high in the roof, and are eight feet deep by twelve feet in length. They are completely undrained; the footpath is the wet clay. There is no supply of water, and the occupants " get it from their neighbours," or " where they can." There is one privy, which has a cesspool in common with a separate privy attached to another house. The cesspool is nearly full; the wood-work of the privy can scarcely hold together, and it is dangerous to use it. Not long ago the landlady of some houses in Armstrong-buildings fell into a cesspool and was suffocated. Such an event is extremely probable here from the dilapidated condition of the place. There is no dust-heap in this place; a sad mark of wretchedness, inasmuch as where there is no dust-heap to be found, it is to be concluded that it is the practice to spread the refuse over the neighbouring soil. The vegetable matter, being mixed with the dust, forms a fresh layer of soil, well adapted for the growth of plants and the destruction of human beings. The occupants of these *houses* are likewise destitute of slop-holes, but throw their foul water into the ditch fronting their houses. It scarcely needs to be remarked that these houses are very damp. They are respectively occupied by two persons, by four persons (a man, two women, and a child), by six persons (a man, woman, and four children), and by one person. 1s. a week is paid as rent for each of these most wretched abodes.

JAMES-PLACE, JAMES-STREET, 44.—Consists of two huts in a filthy yard, with dung and refuse heaped against the wall. The privy is perfectly filthy.

NORTH-PASSAGE, 45.—In this alley garbage and refuse heaps are piled against the wall, and the gutter in the centre is choked with black slime and mud.

HAMDEN'S-PLACE, a continuation of Braemar-street, 46.—The road is excessively dirty.

BRAEMAR-STREET, 47.—The road is broken up, and very dirty.

TABLE ILLUSTRATING SANITARY STATE OF DISTRICT, No. I.

The facts as to Drainage and Sewerage are derived from the parish surveyor, and a corrected map of the Tower Hamlets Commission of Sewers. The state of the Streets and Houses, and the Nuisances, from personal inspection. The deaths from Zymotic diseases, from the the returns to the Register General, and the cases of Zymotic diseases medically treated, from the books of the Parochial Medical officers. Both are for one year, ending October 1st, 1847.

DISTRICT No. I. Streets, Courts, and Alleys, &c.	Number of Houses.	Footpath F.	Footpath Paved P.	Granite Roadway G.	Street Drainage D.	Sewered S.	Streets Clean C.	Sts dirty or very dirty v vd	Gutters full or overflowing.	Privies full or overflowing p f	Nuisances, refer to figures.	Deaths from fever in 12 months	Deaths from other Zymotic dis	Cases of fvr attd by m.d. officer	Cs of other Zymotic dis in 12 ms	Courts C, Alleys A, Cul-de-sacs Cul, Private P, Gardens G.
Baker-st., Green-st		F			D				vd	gf.	p.f	20				
Barnsley-alley, or street												7	3		2	
Bates-place, Jew's Walk		F	P		D	S			d				1			
Behind Chester-place		F			D				vd	gf.		42				Cul.
Bethnal-green East		F	P		D	S.										
Bethnal-green North		F	P		D				d				1			
Bethnal-green West		F	P		D		C			gf.						
Blue Anchor or Russia-lane		F			D				vd	gf.		40		1		
Bernham-square							C					37				
Bonner's-lane, Green-street		F							vd	gf.	pf.	33			6	2	
Bonner-st., Green-street		F							vd	gf.	pf.			1		
Braemar-st., West-street, Green-street		F							vd	gf.		47				
Brown-st., Globe-street		F														

DISTRICT, No. 1.

Streets, Courts, and Alleys.	Number of Houses.	Footpath F.	Footpath Paved P.	Granite Roadway G.	Street Drainage D.	Sewerage S.	Streets Clean C.	Sts dirty or very dirty, v d vv d	Gutters full or overflowing.	Privies full or overflowing pf.	Nuisances refer to figures.	Dths from fvr in 12 months.	Dths from other Zymotic dis.	Cases of fvr attd by mdc. officer.	Cs of othr Zymtic dis in 12 m	Courts C, Alleys A, Cul-de-sacs Cul, Private P. Gardens G.
Bullard's-pl. or Cemetary-pl	..	F	..	..	D	..	..	d	gf.	..	23	..	..	...	1	..
Butler-st., Green-st	..	F	P	..	D	D	S	C	..	gf.	..	..	..	..	..	..	p.s
Cambridge-rd	..	F	P	..	D	D	..	C	..	..	..	1	1	8	3	2	..
Chandlers-ct., Martha-st	2	F	..	..	D	..	..	..	..	..	..	..	..	..	..	..
Charles-ct., King-st., Old-Ford-lane	8	..	..	..	..	..	..	..	d	gf.	..	..	..	3	..	..
Charles-street	..	..	..	..	..	..	..	..	vd	gf.	..	22	..	..	..	..
Charlotte-st., Gretton-pl	..	..	..	..	..	..	..	..	vd	gf.	..	..	..	2	3	1	..
Chester-pl., Green-st	..	F	P	G	D	S	..	d	..	..	..	..	..	..	..	..
Cleveland-st	..	F	P	G	D	S	..	..	..	..	..	..	2	..	..	..
Cross-st., Green-st	..	F	..	..	..	..	..	vd	gf.	pf.	29	1	2	8	2	Cul
Cross-street, Cambridge-rd	..	..	..	..	..	..	..	..	d	gf.	..	10	..	..	..	..
Darling-row, Cambridge-rd	..	F	..	..	D	..	..	vd	gf.	pf.	12	..	..	..	..	..
Digby-st., Globe-rd	..	..	..	..	D	..	..	vd	gf.	pf.	18	..	2	3	2	..
Digby-walk, Globe-rd	..	..	..	..	..	..	..	vd	gf.	pf.	19	..	1	1	..	Alley.
East-st., Prospect-row	..	F	..	..	..	..	..	vd	gf.	..	..	..	..	..	..	..
East-st., Green-st	..	F	..	..	..	..	..	vd	gf.	..	..	..	1	6	2	..
Ely-place, Digby-st., Globe-road	..	F	..	..	D	..	..	vd	gf.	pf.	17	..	2	4	7	Alley.
Essex-st., Northampton-st.	..	F	..	..	..	..	..	vd	gf.	..	13	..	1	..	..	..
Flints-ct., King-st	5	F	..	..	..	..	..	..	gf.	..	..	..	..	..	2	..
Garden-place, James-street	..	F	..	..	D	..	..	vd	..	pf.	16	..	..	4	..	Alley.
George-st., O.B.G.R.	..	F	..	..	D	..	..	vd	gf.	..	2	..	..	4	..	..
Globe-place	..	F	..	..	..	..	..	..	..	..	..	..	..	2	..	..
Globe-road	..	F	P	G	D	S	..	vd	gf.	..	..	..	3	..	..	..
Globe-st	..	..	..	..	..	..	..	..	..	..	..	..	..	2	1	..
Globe-terrace	..	..	..	..	..	..	..	d	gf.	..	..	..	..	..	..	..
Gloucester-st., Cambridge Heath	..	F	..	..	..	..	C	..	..	..	..	1	3	..	..	..
Green-street	..	F	P	..	D	S	C	..	gf.	..	..	2	2	6	5	..
Gretton-place	..	F	P	..	D	..	..	vd	gf.	pf.	..	..	..	..	..	..
Grosvenor-place, Globe-st	..	F	..	..	..	..	..	vd	gf.	..	38	..	1	3	6	..
Hamden's-place, Braemar-st	..	F	..	..	..	..	..	vd	gf.	..	46	..	1	..	..	..
Harrold-st., Green-st	..	F	..	..	..	..	..	d	gf.	pf.	26	1	..	..	..	..
Helen's-place, Chester-place	..	F	..	..	D	..	..	d	gf.	pf.	43	..	..	..	..	Alley
James-ct., James-st	..	F	..	..	..	..	..	..	..	..	..	..	..	..	...	C.
James-place, James-st	..	F	..	..	..	..	..	d	..	pf.	44	..	..	..	..	C.
James-st., Green-st	..	F	..	..	d	..	..	d	gf.	..	16	..	3	1	1	..
John Smart's Court, No. Pavement	3	..	..	..	..	..	..	..	..	..	..	..	..	..	..	P.C.

Streets, Courts, and Alleys, &c. (DISTRICT, No I.)	Number of Houses	Footpath F.	Footpath Paved P.	Granite Roadway G.	Street Drainage D.	Sewerage S	Street Clean C.	Sts. dirty or very dirty d vd.	Gutters full or overflowing g f.	Privies full or overflowing pf.	Nuisances refer to figures.	Deaths from fever in 12 ms.	Dths frm other zymotic dis.	Cass of fvr atdd by med offr.	Cs of Zymotic dis in 12 ms.	Courts C, Alleys A, Cul-de-sacs Cul, Private P, Gardens G.
John-st., Bonner-st		F.										1	1			
John-st., Cambridge-rd		F.	P.		D.			vd	gf.		14	1	1	1		
John-street, Green-st								vd	gf.				11		2	
John's-Ct., James-st	4							d	gf.		15					C.
King-st., Old Ford-lane		F.						vd	gf.		31					
Knottisford-st., Green-st		F.	P.		D.			vd	gf.		21		1			
Lark-row					D.			d					2	6	3	
Little George-st., O.B.G.Rd								d	gf.						2	
Mad House																C.
Martha-ct, Martha-street	13				D.			vd		pf.	42					
Martha-st., Cambridge-heath		F.			D.			d	gf.				4	1		
Mockford's-buildging's	5										5		2			
Morpeth-st., Green-street		F.	P.		D.	S.	C.	vd	gf.		8			1	1	
New Somerford-street								vd	gf.							
Norfolk-street, Cambridge-road		F.						vd	gf.		1		1	1		
Northampton-staeet, Cambridge-rd		F.			D.			vd	gf.		11	1	1			Alley.
North-passage, Green-street		F.						vd	gf.		45					
North-pavement, Green-st		F.						d	gf.		36		1		4	
North-place, Green-street		F.											1	2		
North-st., Globe-street		F.											1			
Norton-street, Green-street		F.						d			32			3		
Old Ford-lane		F.														P.
Palestine-place		F.			D.	S.	C.	d		pf.	4	1		1	2	
Paradise-row, Bethnal-green		F.	P.					vd	gf.		35			3	2	
Park-street		F.						gf.								
Patriot-square		F.	P.		D.		C.	gf.						1	3	Alley.
Peacock-alley, on Bethnal-green, West		F.			D.			vd	gf.	pf.	3		1	8	7	
Pitt-st., Green-st		F.						vd	gf.	pf.	30					
Pleasant-place, Bonner-st		F.											1			
Pleasant-row, Cambridge-rd													3			
Prospect-row		F.	P.		D.			vd	gf.							
Providence-st., Globe-fields		F.														C.
Providence-place, or Blue Anchor-lane					D.			vd	gf.	pf.	39		3	2	3	
Preston-st., Twig Folly		F.			D.			vd	gf.							
Saint James-place		F.	P.		D.											
Salisbury-st.		F.	P.		D.						28		1	5		Cul.
Sydney-st., Green-st		F.						vd	gf.			1	2	3	1	
Smart-st., Green-st		F.			D.			d	gf.							
South Pavement, Green-st		F.						vd	gf.							

DISTRICT, No. I.

Streets, Courts, and Alleys, &c.	Number of Houses.	Footpath F.	Footpath Paved P.	Granite Roadway G.	Street Drainage D.	Sewered S.	Streets Clean C.	Sts dirty or very dirty v vd.	Gutters full or overflowing gf.	Privies full or overflowing pf.	Nuisances, refer to figures.	Deaths from fever in 12 ms.	Dths frm other zymodtic dis	Cas of fvr attd by med offir.	Cas of zymotic dis in 12 ms.	Courts C, Alleys A, Cul-de-sacs Cul, Private P, Gardens G.
Suffolk-st., Northampton-st	F.							vd	gf.		6		4			
Sugar Loaf Walk				D				d								Alley.
Surat-place, Smart-street	F.	P		D	D		C							1	1	
Thomas-st., Cambridge-rd	F.				D				d	gf.		1	4			Cul.
Toplis-ct., North Pavement																Alley.
Type-st., Green-street	F.							vd	gf.	pf.	27		4	2	6	
Violet-row	F.							vd	gf.		25		1			Alley.
West-street, do	F.				D			vd	gf.		24			2	2	
West-st., Prospect-row								d	gf.							
Whiskers Gardens									gf.	pf.	34	1	1	2		G.
Whitechapel-rd., from M.E Gate to Wentworth's Fac.	F.	P		D	S.											
William-st., Green-street	F.				D				d	gf.		1	1	1	1	
Workhouse												7	32	363		

DISTRICT, No. 2.

This district contains very few good houses, with the exception of those in Bethnal-green-road, and Pollard's-row. The great majority of the other houses are the abodes of those a little above the poor, and the poor following every variety of occupation. A very considerable proportion of the inhabitants are weavers; a W is attached to the names of those streets chiefly occupied by weavers. One of the peculiarities of this district is, that between Bethnal-green-road and Three Colt-lane, more particularly, but likewise in other parts of the district, there are great numbers of isolated houses, huts, or sheds placed on the ground, with plots of ground in front of, and surrounding them. These were formerly, that is to say, from forty years ago, downwards to the present day, summer-houses surrounded with plots of ground, and used as places of floriculture and recreation by the citizens of London. Hence these places are called gardens. The tide of citizen emigration has for a long time however, been diverted from Bethnal-green, and the wooden sheds and temporary huts erected on the bare soil, for storing gardening utensils, and in which to spend the summer evenings, have gradually been converted into human habitations. None, or almost none of the houses which are now on the ground, were originally intended for the dwellings of human beings, but for the purposes specified. The commencement of this transition state is to be observed in Whisker's-gardens, District No. 1. The entrance to these abodes is by narrow lanes, which are unpaved, and consequently nearly always muddy, in wet weather more particularly so, so that ingress or egress is necessarily accompanied with personal uncleanness. These dwellings, in some instances, are unfit to house cattle in; in other, but very few instances (I think I could count the exceptions), they are tolerably clean. They are totally without drainage of any kind, except into shallow cesspools, or holes dug in the gardens; they are consequently extremely damp, and the inhabitants suffer much from rheumatism, from febrile diseases, from diseases of the respiratory and digestive organs, from nervous affections, and cachexia. There is very seldom any water laid on to the houses; one stand-tap, as in Middle-walk, George-gardens, generally supplies five, ten, or sixteen houses. Many houses are altogether without water, and the inhabitants require to get it as they best can. In Wilmot-grove the peculiarity of barrels sunk in the ground is to be remarked. Some of the houses have wells, as in Camden-gardens. Very few of these houses have regular cesspools; the privies are sometimes placed close beside the entrance to the house, at other times at the extremity of the garden bordering the narrow lane or footpath. They are, in the majority of cases, full, in some instances, overflowing, and frequently, like the houses themselves, in a dilapidated condition. Another peculiarity in this district, is the number of alleys and narrow lanes, many of them forming cul-de-sacs. The houses in these alleys are always of the very worst description, and are in an excessively dirty state. There is seldom any house drainage, or if there be, it is only to a gutter in front, where the water stagnates, till the sun's heat shall cause it to disappear by evaporation. It is the nearly universal custom to throw the refuse water and garbage on the streets.

This district seems to be capable of very great amelioration; there is sufficient space to ensure free and complete ventilation; there are no piles of buildings to cause the air to stagnate, or to seduce a multitude of occupants into a contracted space. The soil is gravelly, and is not opposed to natural drainage. The evils which exist in it are evidently of man's formation, and are clearly traceable to negligence and indifference on the part of the owners of property to the wants and necessities of the poor;—huts and sheds metamorphosed into houses—two-roomed houses planted on the damp soil, without drainage or sewerage,—without a sufficient supply of water—with no decent accommodation for the demands of nature—with no receptacles for refuse, and no provision whatever for removing it—with general cleansing utterly neglected—and all sorts of nuisances tolerated, in spite of demonstration and reprobation. These are the phenomena which strike the reflecting observer.

The following are the details of my investigations into the condition of this district, and the result of my personal inspections;—

GALE'S-GARDENS, 1.—Collections of heaped dung and vegetable refuse, oyster-shells, &c., encumber the narrow entrance to these gardens; near the Bethnal-green-road some swine are kept, and the place is very filthy; in one part there are 10 families supplied from one tap, to which on all occasions they must go.

HOLLY-BUSH-GARDENS, 2.—A lead-factory is situated here.

CAMDEN-GARDENS, 3.—The houses in these gardens are brick buildings, with some wooden sheds; they are placed on the damp ground, and have generally two rooms on the ground floor; the gardens are similar to those in Whisker's-gardens, but have been partly converted into dust-yards. The houses vary in size from seven feet by nine, to a large dog-kennel; they are very rarely higher than seven feet. At the entrance to these gardens there is a cow-shed; there are also in the gardens pig-styes, the refuse from which is dug into the gardens, to promote the fecundity of the ground. There is no supply of water except by wells; the smell arising from various parts of this place is very offensive; the total want of drainage renders the paths dirty and muddy, the houses damp, and the inmates unhealthy. There is occasionally fever here, although not always prevalent; when it once gets into a house, it generally affects every member of the family.

THREE COLT-LANE, 4.—A sewer has at last been just laid down by the late Tower Hamlet's Commission as far as Hinton-street; the road is in the worst possible condition, being ploughed up, and very filthy. A row of new houses, called Alpha-row, has sprung up on the north side of the Railway; and on the south side of the Railway 22 new houses are nearly completed. It is between these two rows of houses that the filthy and notorious ditch in Lamb's-fields is situated. The Commissioners, in laying down a new sewer in Three Colt-lane, were chiefly actuated by the outcries which had been raised against them for permitting the continuance of a nuisance in Lamb's-fields, almost, if not quite, unparalleled, as an outrage against a social community. The following was the state of this nuisance when I visited it on several occasions, about three months ago:—" In place of about 300 square feet, as described by Dr. Southwood Smith nine years ago, being covered with putrid water, I found that all the space enclosed between a boarding on either side of the Eastern Counties Railway, and extending from part of Arch 91, and the half of Arch 92, up to the end of Arch 98, a distance of about 230 feet, and from 40 to 60 feet in width, was one enormous ditch or stagnant lake of thickened putrefying matter; in this Pandora's box dead cats and dogs were profusedly scattered, exhibiting every stage of disgusting decomposition. Leading into this lake was a foul streamlet, very slowly flowing, and from it another, which widened and expanded into a large ditch before it disappeared in the open end of a sewer. Bubbles of carburetted and sulphuretted hydrogen gas, and every pestilential exhalation resulting from putrefaction, were being most abundantly given off from the ditches and the lake. The ripples on the surface of water occasioned by a shower of rain are not more numerous than were those produced by the bursting of the bubbles of these pestilential gases which were about to produce disease and death. The construction of the Railway has diminished the extent of this lake, but it has *concentrated* the evil. Now the concentration of such foci of disease has been proved to be deleterious in a geometrically increasing ratio. What, therefore, must be the effect of this lake of putrescency on the health and lives of those who shall inhabit the houses that are rapidly springing up all around it. A row of 22 new houses of two flats, with cesspools in front, are being built parallel to, and within 10 feet of this most disgusting and degrading scene, which is an abomination dangerous even to the casual inspector."—*Lecture*, pp. 23, 24. A deep ditch has been dug on either side of the Railway by the Company, into which a considerable part of the semi-fluid fœtid pestilential matter has drained. These ditches were dug by the Company to prevent the foundations of the arches being endangered, and are in no ways to be considered as having been dug to promote the health of the neighbourhood. The double privies attached to the new houses on the south side are immediately contiguous to this ditch, and are constructed so that the night-soil shall drain into it. For this purpose the cesspools are small, and the bottoms are above the level of the ditch. It appears, therefore, that after the public have laid down a sewer, in order that this horrid lake of putrescency might be drained, it is intended that the ditches shall be retained, and that they shall be rendered, if possible, still more deadly and abominable, by the copious addition of night-soil. The solution of this apparently inexplicable problem is to be found in the immunity which attaches to the perpetration of such outrages, and the callous avarice and atrocious selfishness which prefer that the public shall suffer from such outrages till they choose, at their own expense, to deliver themselves from their destructive operation. The reputed owner of this property is not free from the suspicion that these nuisances are encouraged, in order to throw the burden of their suppression on the public. It is impossible to speak in terms sufficiently strong to convey an adequate impression of the disgust occasioned by this nuisance. That part of Three Colt-lane which is without a sewer is very dirty, and the gutters full of dirt and fluid filth. There is always a great deal of fever in this lane. Parallel to, and north of, Arch 81 of the Railway, and abutting on the lane, is a small pool of pasty putrescent filth, and a collection of garbage. On the south side of the same arch is an open filthy black ditch, which is from eight to ten feet wide, and from three to four hundred feet long. The uncovered privies at the back of North-street drain their soil into it; the soil has accumulated, and with decomposing cats and dogs, and refuse, which are now thrown into it, since Lamb's-fields have been occupied, produce an odour of the most abominable character. The place is most disgusting, but the smell is, if possible, worse. A similar ditch, but upon a smaller scale, extends in a northern line from Arch No. 68. Fever is generally extremely prevalent here.

LAMB'S-GARDENS, 5.—Now an open space. There are collections of dung and refuse scattered about.

PRIMROSE-PLACE, 6.—The corner house is occupied by a bladder-drier. An offensive odour is occasionally given off from these premises.

TENT-ST., 7, has a pretty large open space between it and the Railway, but in the centre of it there is a collection of stagnant water.

SMART'S-GARDENS, 8.—There are filthy collections of dung and dirt here.

SCOTT-ST., 9.—The backs of the houses on the south side have the privies under their windows. There is generally fever prevailing here.

PLEASANT-ROW, 10, and PLEASANT-PLACE, 11.—Pleasant-row forms the northern side; Pleasant-place the eastern and southern sides of a quadrangular space, opposite the Jews' burying-ground. In the centre of this space is a smaller square, leaving a narrow passage to the east side of the square, and a still narrower passage to the southern; it is continuous with the western boundary. This central square is made up of swine-pens and yards in which dung-heaps are piled; in it are the privies of the northern half of the row, forming the south of the square. Immediately facing Pleasant-row is a ditch, filled with slimy mud and putrefying filth, which extends for 100 feet. The space between Pleasant-row and the central square is, beyond description, filthy; dung-heaps and putrefying garbage, refuse, and manure, fill up the horrid place, which is covered with slimy fœtid mud. The eastern end has likewise its horrid filthy fœtid gutter reeking with pestilential effluvia; the southern alley is likewise abominably filthy: there, the same slime and mud overspreads the broken up, bouldered path; and there, the same most disgusting odours are given off, which are common to this area of putrescence. I do not think that in all my journeyings through the degraded haunts of wretched poverty in this poor parish I have found a scene so distressing. The houses in Pleasant-place are chiefly two-roomed, and let at 3s. 6d. a week, but some of the two-roomed and all the three-roomed houses let at 5s. a week. I entered one of these houses on the southern side, and found that every individual in a family of seven had been attacked with fever, and that a daughter, aged 22, who had been convalescent eight weeks, on her return from the country to her miserable home, died of a relapse in two days. The body was retained in the house, because no means could be found to raise the money necessary to bury it, and was then lying in its coffin. The privy of this house is close to it, and is full and overflowing, covering the yard with its putrescent filth; the stench was perfectly unendurable; the house itself was most shockingly dirty. 3s. a week were paid for this den of pestilence, while the husband and wife together, by working night and day, could only earn 15s. a week. To permit a continuance of the state of things I saw would be, as it were, voluntarily to tolerate the elimination of a fatal poison to be sucked in at every breath of the occupants, who, thus condemned to death, perish not by the momentary pangs of official strangulation, but by the more miserable death of loathsome typhus. How lost to all sense of charity and brotherly love, how forgetful of the value of human life, are those who apathetically survey such sad scenes of wretched misery.

COLLINGWOOD-ST., 12.—This street is divided into two portions, the one containing 20, the other 22 houses; the latter are smaller than the former; the rents are 2s. 6d. and 3s. 6d. a week. In the first division, four of the houses have no supply of water; to obtain it the occupants must beg, or, as they commonly term it, borrow it of their neighbours, who subject themselves to a penalty of 5l. for suplying it. A stand-pipe supplies the first 10 houses: this stand-pipe is the cause of much quarrelling for turns; it is frequently left running, and annoys the person who resides next to it. Fever of a bad character generally prevails here.

The following Table, supplied to me by my friend Mr. Taylor, the medical officer of the district, shows the number of persons sleeping in one room, the dimensions, and the times when death would result from the respiration of the air defiled and rendered poisonous by breathing (provided there were no ventilation, a thing extremely common in the houses of the poor).

No.	Height, 6 feet 7 inches.	Length, 9 feet 7 inches.	Breadth, 9 feet 5 inches.	No. of Persons	Death in	No.	Height, 7 feet 9 inches.	Length, 9 feet 11 inches.	Breadth, 9 feet 5 inches.	No. of persons	Death in
					h. m.						h. m.
1				8	6 47	1				......	—
2				6	9 2	2				5	9 45
3				4	13 34	3				5	9 45
4				2	27 7	4				6	8 7
5				empty	- -	5				3	16 14
6				6	9 2	6				10	4 52
7				5	10 51	7				......	—
8				6	9 2	8				6	8 7
9				2	27 7	9				5	9 46
10				7	7 45	10				3	16 14
12				3	18 5	11				5	9 45
14				6	9 2	12					—
15				5	10 51	13				6	8 7
16				6	9 2	14				5	9 45
17				2	27 7	15				5	9 45
18				6	9 2	16				8	6 5
19				4	13 34	17				7	6 58
20				2	27 7	18				4	12 11
21				7	7 45	19				7	6 58
22				5	10 51	20				7	6 58
						21				9	5 25
						22				6	8 7

This Table is calculated on each respiration consuming 40 cubic inches (Menzies)
  ,, ,, 20 respirations per minute (Haller.)
·08 of carbonic acid gas in the atmosphere being destructive to life (Liebig).

In the calculation no allowance is made for the space occupied by the bed and other furniture, which would materially diminish the volume of air contained in the room. This will counterbalance the amount of air which might enter into, and escape from the room through imperfect ventilation.

SOUTHAMPTON STREET. 13.—Has some stagnant water by the side of the railway.

BECKFORD-ROW, 14.—A narrow confined row of 16 houses with small plots in front. On the south side, they form the northern half of the houses in Alfred-row. The half houses which are in Beckford-row, consist of 2 rooms, one above the other, each room being generally occupied by a separate family. The place is *abominably filthy;* the drains from the houses into a kind of central gutter, are choked up. The privies are full, exposed, and overflowing, and the soil covers the front plots, in which heaps of filth are accumulated. 3s. 6d. and 3s. a week are paid for these miserable habitations. In 14 weeks, 13 cases of fever occurred, and one case of erysipelas. Eight cases of fever occurred in one house. Threee persons slept in the lower room, five in the upper; two cases occurred in the opposite house, and three a few doors further off. There is only one stand-tap to supply water to these houses. The reservoir to contain the supply which takes place for two hours three times a-week, is a small barrel 21 inches in diameter, and 12 deep.

THOMAS-ROW, 15.—A continuation of the above; is nearly in a similar state. There are two dung-heaps in it.

HAGUE-STREET, 16.—Between Mape-street and Hague-street there is a large and deep hollow, in the shape of an irregular triangle, with the sides measuring respectively about 130, 130, and 100 feet. In wet weather this is a sort of pond; into it are thrown at all times the contents of the fish baskets, the heads and intestines of fish, and every kind of animal and vegetable refuse. In the hot and dry weather in which I visited it, the surface had become exsiccated, and the nature of the filthy soil on which I trod was not readily perceived by the eye, but the sense of smell detected, in a concentrated form, the essence of putrefying odours, and the stomach heaved with nausea. At one end of this triangle, and on a level with its lowest surface, are rows of two houses, with open privies, and the soil oozing into a little ditch in the hollow.

HAGUE-PLACE, 17.—There is a collection of dung at the end of this place.

MANCHESTER-PASSAGE, 18.—A row of five houses leading from the south side of Derbyshire-street. Five feet in front of these one-storied, two-roomed houses, is dead wall—it is a blind alley. The alley is two feet above the level of the floor, and is unpaved. The back yards are about six feet, by the breadth of the house, and are from 20 to 30 inches above the level of the floors. In these yards are piled collections of dung, refuse, garbage, and filth. In No. 5, the soil from the privies had soaked into the refuse in the yard, and all the soakage from the yard to below the boarded floor. In No. 4, the boards of the floor were up in consequence of their having become rotten, (through the agency of the excremental soakage,) and were being re-laid by the poor occupant. No. 3 was equally filthy.

Nos. 2 and 1 were occupied by a family of mat makers; two donkeys participated with them the enjoyment of this wretched abode. The back yards of these two houses were remarkable for their accumulation of filth, dung, &c., and had no privies; the excrements were lying about the surface of the yard. 2s. 6d. a-week were paid by the occupants of Nos. 1, 2, and 3; 3s. 3d. by those of Nos. 4 and 5, making a return of 10s. 9d. weekly. The weekly returns of the occupants of No. 5, were about 16s.; of the widow in No. 3, 6s.; and of those of Nos. 2 and 1, 12s. a-week. There is no drainage whatever to these houses; neither is there any supply of water. The inhabitants must get it as they best can, at a distance of several streets. It is needless to observe that water could not be preserved in a state of purity, for even a very short time in such a horrid den.

WILMOT-GROVE, 19.—In these gardens the water is laid on in a somewhat peculiar manner. Small barrels are sunk in the ground, and these are filled from the Company's pipes thrice a-week, when the usual supply comes on.

GEORGE-GARDENS, 20.—Gardens with similar two-roomed houses; the lane is generally muddy and dirty. The privies are close upon the windows.

GEORGE-ROW, 21.—These gardens are similar in all respects to the others; only, that one barrel or reservoir supplies a number of separate houses and families,—five or more.

FALCON-COURT, OR HENLEY-PLACE, 22.—The first house has no water-supply, and there is a collection of refuse and dung in it.

ABBEY-PLACE, 23.—There is no water-supply to these houses, except from a common pump.

DERBYSHIRE-ST., WEST, 24.—Since the publication of my Lecture, and the appeals made to some of the Members of the Cleansing Board, part of this street has been drained, and the surface made somewhat level. The following is a statement of the condition in which it was. " Derbyshire-street runs parallel with Bethnal-green-road; the one side, that nearest the road, is higher than the opposite. For the length of about 260 feet there is a gutter and deep hollow, filled with stagnant and putrefying filthy fluid. When wet weather comes, this fluid, filth, is washed into the houses on the opposite side of the street, and inundates them, leaving when it subsides a compost of mud and filth. The continuation of Derbyshire-street to the east, called Alfred-row, has on its north side the privies bordering the foot-path. These are broken down, and the soil oozes from them, and finds a resting-place in the gutter by the side." Lecture pp. 24, 25.

This part of the street is, however, still very dirty; collections of garbage and decomposing vegetables are abundantly strewed about, so that there is still a considerable accumulation of fluid muddy filth in the gutter; but there appears much less danger of the opposite houses being inundated with the pestilential slime on the occurrence of rains.

DERBYSHIRE-STREET, EAST, OR ALFRED-ROW, however, has undergone no change; the street is very filthy and dirty; the gutters still full of black putrid filth, which overflows the road; the privies still drain into the gutters; filth still abounds. Fever and erysipelas are common in this street. At the eastern end of the northern side of the street, called Alfred-row, which constitutes the back of the wretched hovels, called Beckford-row, there is an accumulation of dung, filth, and piles of refuse which drain into the soil and render the place *most abominably filthy*. The odour from this neighbourhood was scarcely endurable. There is no water-supply to these houses, but the inhabitants require to provide themselves with it from a stand-tap adjoining, and under the same roof as the privies. I entered the two last houses in this row—the houses being composed of two rooms, one above the other, each occupied by different families. The size of the lower rooms of these houses is 10-feet 1-inch, by 11-feet, (allowing for a recess,) and 6-feet 9-inches in height. In the last house the atmosphere was scarcely to be breathed, even for a moment, with impunity. Four persons sleep in it. Two children had had small-pox, of whom one died; the other was at the height of the eruption. In the second last house, the air was equally foul—six persons sleep in the apartment. Four persons had had small-pox, of these three had been vaccinated, but the vaccination had not taken in one, who died with confluent eruption. The fourth was a babe, then exhibiting the disease in an aggravated form.

PITT-ST., 25.—Has a slaughter-house at the top, and an extensive piggery near the centre of the street. The place is very damp, and quite undrained.

POTT-ST., 96.—Collections of mud on either side of the street, preparatory to removal.

LUCAS-ST., 27.—Collections of mud, as above. At the west-end of the street is a marine-store dealer, from whose premises there frequently arises the most offensive smells; at the east end there is an extensive piggery.

COVENTRY-ST., 28.—Collections of mud as above.

BATH-ST., 29.—Similar collections of mud.

BATH-PLACE, 30.—This court is supplied with water from two barrells below a stand-pipe.

PARLIAMENT-PLACE, 31.—There are four miserable houses in this court. The rooms are 7-ft. high, 10½-feet long, by 10-feet 2-inches deep; and they are supplied with water from a cock in the wall. There is one privy in a dilapidated filthy state in the court, open to all passers-bye; the soil oozes into the surface-drain which is stopped, rendering the place very dirty.

PARLIAMENT-COURT, 32.—In two of these 2-roomed houses, the rooms of which are 7-feet 8-inches high, by 10-feet 6-inches in height, and 9-feet 7-inches in breadth, nine persons sleep. According to Mr. Taylor's calculation, these persons would perish from the respiration of the poisonous air produced by their own breathing, in seven hours. The pressure of the water is so insufficient, that the two last houses in this court are very badly supplied.

PARLIAMENT-ST,, 33.—There are mud collections as already referred to. The gutters in some places are full of very filthy fœtid matter.

ABINGDON-COURT, 34.—A cock in the wall supplies these four houses with water, for which £2 per annum are paid by the landlord. The houses are two roomed; 2s. and 2s. 6d. a week are paid for them. In one a man and his wife by their labour earn 12s. 6d, a-week, and support themselves and two children, after paying their rent. The last house, in this court has the wall infiltrated, and the ground below the floor wet, with the fluid which has drained from a neighbouring cesspool; the inmate is ill, and the landlord grievously complains of the injury done to his property.

JUBILEE-PLACE, 35.—A court entering from Parliament-street by a narrow passage. There are 8 houses in this court, each 2-roomed. There is one stand-tap, from which, when the supply comes on, the inhabitants have each to fill their small barrels. There are two privies, nearly full, common to the court; there is no back-yard ; there is no dust-bin, and, consequently, there is nearly always a considerable accumulation of refuse, garbage, &c. piled against the well; this is seldom removed. The houses Nos. 3 and 4 have a drain under the floor, the effluvia from which cause them to smell very offensively. The paint by the action of the sulphuretted hydrogen gas emitted, is turned black. The court is never cleansed, because it is private property. There is no house-drainage; there is a small surface-drain in the court, which is stopped up. The place is very dirty. 2s. 6d. a-week are paid for these houses, the rooms of which are 10-feet 5-inches long, 9-feet 10-inches broad, and 6-feet 9-inches high. One family of six persons living in one house earned 7s. 6d. a-week; another family of six persons, all sleeping in one room, earned 15s. a-week; whilst a third family of seven persons could only earn at present 3s. a-week.

Mr. Taylor has favoured me with the following Table, similar to that under the head of Little Collingwood-street.

No.				No. of persons.	Death in
1				6	9 . 27
2				1	56 . 42
3	6-feet 9-inches—height.	10-feet 5-inches—length.	9-feet 10-inches—breadth.	3	18 . 54
4				3	18 . 54
5				9	6 . 18
6				7	8 . 6
7				6	9 . 27
8				8	7 . 6

COLLINGWOOD-TERRACE, 36.—A very disagreeable and offensive odour is given off from this street. The house at which I casually inquired had an inmate just dead of fever.

ELIZABETH-PLACE, 37.—This filthy wretched place has 14 houses in it. Stagnant fœtid filth perpetually covers the bouldered footway. Excrements and garbage quite disgusting fill up one entrance, while at the extremity dung-heaps and fœtid refuse are boarded up. 3s. a week are paid for these pestilential abodes. The inhabitants in one house earned 15s., in another 10s., in another 7s. or 8s., and in another 4s. or 5s. weekly. Six of these beastly dens were empty, most fortunately. As the entrances to this place are extremely narrow, and the place itself extremely contracted, ventilation is in the worst possible state. But that seems only in keeping with the whole character of the locality, and its squalid, wretched inhabitants. This place is quite unfit for human existence.

CHARLES-ST., 38.—At the boundary of the parish in this street, and partly within it, and partly in the parish of Whitechapel, is an extensive dairy or cowshed, in a most offensive state. The soil was collected in a large wooden tank, and the surface of the whole place covered with decomposing refuse. The smell from the place was most offensive and disgusting. It was impossible to walk along this, or the neighbouring streets (the wind blowing from the S.W.) without nausea arising from the sickening and offensive odours wafted from the neighbouring collection of night-soil, and patent manure manufactory. Though they are out of the parish, still, as the health of the inhabitants is affected by them, I introduce the following description of them. "On the western side of Spitalfields workhouse, and entered from a street, called Queen-street, is a nightman's yard. A heap of dung and refuse of every description, about the size of a pretty large house, lies piled to the left of the yard; to the right, is an artificial pond, into which the contents of cesspools are thrown. The contents are allowed to desiccate in the open air; and they are frequently stirred for that purpose. The odour which was given off when the contents were raked up, to give me an assurance that there was nothing so very bad in the alleged nuisance, drove me from the place with the utmost speed I was master of. On two sides of this horrid collection of excremental matter, was a patent manure manufactory. To the right in this yard, was a large accumulation of dung, &c.; but, to the left, there was an extensive layer of a compost of blood, ashes, and nitric acid, which gave out the most horrid, offensive, and disgusting concentration of putrescent odours it has ever been my lot to be the victim of. The whole place presented a most foul and filthy aspect, and an example of the enormous outrages which are perpetrated in London against society. It is a curious fact, that the parties who had charge of these two premises were each dead to the foulness of their own most pestilential nuisances. The nightman's servant accused the premises of the manure manufacturer as the source of perpetual foul smells, but thought his yard free from any particular cause of complaint; while the servant of the patent manure manufacturer diligently and earnestly asserted the perfect freedom of his master's yard from foul exhalations; but considered that the raking up of the drying night-soil, on the other side of the wall, was "quite awful, and enough to kill anybody." Immediately adjoining the patent manure manufactory is the establishment of a bottle-merchant. He complained to me in the strongest terms of the expenses and annoyances he had been put to through the emanations which floated in the atmosphere having caused his bottles to spoil the wine which was bottled in bottles that had not been *very* recently washed. He was compelled frequently to change his straw, and frequently to wash his bottles, and considered that, unless the nuisance could be suppressed, he would be compelled to leave his present premises. Since the publication of my lecture, the atrocious nuisance of the Patent Manure Manufacturer has been suppressed; although the soil then on the ground was valued at £2000. But as similar nuisances, at the present time exist in some parts of Bethnal Green parish, and are not likely to be removed either voluntarily or compulsarily, the evidence of the parochial medical officer, given to the police magistrate, will be eminently serviceable in explaining the deadly influences of such foci of disease. " In Spitalfields workhouse, scarcely 100 yards distant from the nuisance, febrile and other affection considerably prevailed, these were greatly induced by the contiguity of the manufactory, as whenever the wind blew from the premises, it carried an odour in the highest degree offensive, and calculated to produce the most pernicious consequences. On such occasions whatever diseases happened to prevail in the workhouse exhibited a great tendency to *putrescence*, and assumed a most malignant and untractable character. Four hundred children were contained in the house, who were more susceptible than adults to the effects of an impure state of the atmosphere, and amongst these there had lately broke out no less than 12 cases of *spontaneous gangrene*, a disease which but very rarely existed unless the atmosphere was very impure, and the whole of these cases had terminated fatally. Whenever the effluvium became powerful, the adult portion of the inmates were invariably attacked with diarrhœa of the worst form." On referring to Digby-street, p. 9, the importance and practical bearing of these remarks will be fully apparent.

PUNDERSON'S-GARDENS, 39.—Dr. Southwood Smith gives us the following description of Punderson's-gardens in 1838;—" Punderson's-gardens is a long narrow street, in the centre of which is an open rush-gutter, in which filth of every kind is allowed to accumulate and putrefy. A mud-bank, on each side, commonly keeps the contents of this gutter in their situation; but sometimes, and especially in wet weather, the gutter overflows; its contents are then poured into the neighbouring houses, and the street is rendered nearly impassable. The privies are close upon the footpath of the street, being separated from it only by a paling of wood: the street is wholly without drainage of any kind. Fever constantly breaks out in it, and extends from house to house. It has lately been very prevalent here, and we have had several fatal cases from it in the London Fever Hospital." On several occasions lately I have visited this locality, as well in wet, as in dry weather. The only change which has been made in it, during the last twenty-three years, is declared by an old inhabitant to have been for the worse. In place of the gutter in the centre of the roadway, there is now a road, and a gutter on either side. These gutters are always full, even after long-continued dry weather, because the inhabitants have no where else to throw their refuse water. In wet weather the road is nearly impassable; the soil from the privies soaks into the gutters, and the whole refuse from a large pig-stye is every morning swept into it. As if to concentrate the evil still further, there are large cow-sheds and pig-styes close by, from which very nauseous odours were given off. It is right, however, that I should state, that Punderson's Garden i by no means worthy of the bad eminence which has been thrust upon it; I hav seen in nearly every part of the parish of Bethnal Green places in a mnch worse condition than Punderson's Garden.

BETHNAL-GREEN-ROAD, 40.—Except in three small patches, not altogether amounting to more than a few yards, this street, forming the main road in the parish for 1,700 yards, is altogether without a sewer. The Commissioners could not plead ignorance of that fact, because for many years they had been repeatedly memorialized, and the following circumstance brought under their notice, namely that the cellars of the houses do not extend to the depth of 3 feet 6 inches below the depth of the carriage-way, and that there is an average depth of 18 inches of water in them during the greater part of the winter season, compelling many persons to use the pump for many hours daily to preserve their property. (George Reynolds, Registrar.) In many of the gardens or back-yards attached to the houses, especially those towards the eastern end of the road, water is come upon in digging to a depth of only 18 inches. This road is likewise drained very badly, it is consequently nearly always excessively dirty, even although it is the main road, and the most frequently cleansed of any in the parish. A great part of it has lately had an excellent granite roadway laid down, which is in very good condition. It will, of course, be necessary to take up this roadway when a sewer shall be made (and it is incredible that the inhabitants can much longer tolerate the present condition of things, produced by the want of a sewer) The roadway thus taken up well not be as well laid down again; the road will be spoiled, and the expense of taking it up and putting it down again must be incurred. The gutters of this road are always full, and garbage of all descriptions are constantly being thrown on it. Unless for the frequent cleansing it would soon become as filthy as any of the filthiest streets in the parish; as it is, a great part of it is constantly very dirty. In this road there are numerous slaughter-houses, and various nuisances, among these may be mentioned a marine-store-dealer, whose yard presents a most horrid accumulation of all kinds of dirty matters.

GROVE-ST., CAMDEN-GARDENS, 41.—This place is covered with garbage from the putrefaction of which the most offensive odours arise, sensibly affecting every passer-by. This street is in a most disgraceful condition.

NEW YORK-ST, 42.—The back-yards of the houses in this street are small, damp, and filthy. Holes are dug in the ground into which to throw the refuse, slops, and foul water.

CAMBRIDGE-ST., 43.—A blind alley, with a dead wall in front. There is no proper footpath, and the place is very damp. There is however, a tap and a privy to each house, and the usual accumulation of dirt, dust, and garbage. In the first house I find all the small tubs filled with water, and exposed in the yard to the emanations from the refuse heaps and privies. The houses have three rooms and a small wash-house. The rent is 5s. 6d. a week.

WOLVERLEY-ST., 44—At the end of this street, and abutting on a brick-field, the road is in a muddy state, and resembles a stagnant pool covered with green slime.

NORTH CONDUIT-ST., 45.—This street is in a dirty condition; at the northern end a surface-drain leads into the neighbouring brick-field.

SEABRIGHT-ST., 46.—On this street are several heaps of rubbish and refuse. In it there is a cow-yard, but only on a small scale; there is, nevertheless, the usual collections of offensive animal remains and decomposing vegetable matter. This street is filled with weavers.

CROSSLAND or GROSVENOR-PL., SALE-ST., 17.—A row of 12 houses, with a footpath in front three feet below the level of the road; they are, consequently, very damp and confined.

CROSSLAND or GROSVENOR-SQUARE, 48.—Ten houses in a kind of court planted on the damp undrained soil, presenting a rheumatic aspect.

ST. ANDREW'S-ST., 49.—An open space at the end of this street is, as yet, unbuilt upon, and is used as a convenient place on which to deposit dust, dirt, refuse, and garbage of all sorts.

FOSTER-ST., 50.—This street contains 24 houses; the size of the rooms in which the occupants sleep is 6 feet 10 inches high, and 9 feet 2 inches deep. In five of these houses four persons sleep in one room, in six houses five persons in one room, in one house nine persons in one room, and in one house ten persons in one room. By Mr. Taylor's calculations, these persons must perish from the foul air of their own begetting, in the respective periods of 13h. 2m., 10h. 29m., 5h. 48m., and 5h. 13m.

DISTRICT, No. 2.

Streets, Courts, and Alleys, &c.	Number of Houses	Footpath F.	Footpath Paved P.	Granite Roadway G.	Street Drainage D.	Sewerage S.	Streets Clean C.	Sts. dirty or very dry d. vd.	Gutters full or overflowing gf.	Privies full or overflowing pf.	Nuisances refer to figures.	Dths from fvr in 12 months	Dths from other zymotic dis.	Cases of fvr attd by med offr.	Cs of othr Zymtc dis in 12 m	Courts C, Alleys A, Cul-de-sacs Cul. Private P. Gardens G.
Abingdon-court	4	F	P		D						34					Alley
Abingdon-street		F			D				d	gf				2		
Abbey-place	11										23			2		
Albion-street		F	P		D		C			gf				2	1	
Alfred-row, Mape-street		F							vd	gf	pf	24			1	3	Alley
Ann-street, Pollard-row		F	P		D				d	gf						
Arabella-row, Wilmot-grove	W	F					C			gf						
Arundel-street		F	P		D		C						1			Ily
Bath-place		F			D		C			gf		30				C.
Bath-street		F	P		D	S			d	gf		29		1	2	
Beckford-row, Mape-street									vd	gf	pf	14	1	2	15	3	Alley.
Bennett's-place					D		C									Alley.
Beth-gn-rd, Est of White-st		F	P		D				d			40	2	2	1	1	
Cambridge-street	W	18							d		pf	43		1	5	1	Alley.
Camden-gardens									d	gf		3					G Alley
Camden-street	W	F							d	gf					2	
Cheshire-street,	W	F			D				vd	gf						
Collingwood-street					D				vd	gf		12	2	2	4	
Collingwood-terrace		F			D				vd	gf		36		2	1	
Collingwood-place		F			D				d							
Coventry-street		F							d			28	1	3		2	Alley
Coventry-place		F							d							Alley.
Crossland-place Sale-st	W	12	F									47		1	1	2	Alley.
Cross-st., Parliament-st							C							2	1	
Cumberland-place, North-st	3								vd	gf						1	Alley.
Charles-street		F	P									38					
Derbyshire-street		F	P		D				vd	gf		24		2	2	4	
Duke-street, North-street		F	P	G	D	S			vd	gf						1	
Essex-street, Beth Green-rd		F	P	G	D	S			d	gf			3	2	4	7	
Elizabeth Place, Camden-st	14								vd	gf	pf	37			1		Cul.
Foster-street	W	F					C					50				2	
Fox-street	W	F			D		C									Alley.
Gale-gardens									d		pf	1			1		G Alley
George-gardens	W										pf	20		3	2	3	G Alley
George-row									d	gf	pf	21	1				G Alley
Grove-street, or Place									vd	gf		41				1	
Grosvenor-square, Sale-st	W	10	F						d			48	1				
Hague-street					D							16					C.
Hague Place									d	gf		17				2	Alley
Henley, or Falcon-court	W									gf		22	1				Alley.

DISTRICT, No. 2.

Streets, Courts, and Alleys, &c.	Number of Houses	Footpath F.	Footpath Paved P.	Granite Roadway G.	Street Drainage D.	Sewerage S.	Street Clean C.	Sts. dirty or very dirty vd.	Gutters full or ovrflowing gf.	Privies full or overflowing pf.	Nuisances refer to figures.	Deaths from fever in 12 ms.	Dths frm other zymotic dis.	Cass of fvr attd by med offic.	Cs of Zymotic dis in 12 ms.	Courts C, Alleys A, Cul-de-sacs Cul, Private P, Gardens G.
Hinton-street		F.						d	gf.		17				2	Alley.
Hollybush-place		F.			D.			vd	gf.							Alley.
Holybush-gardens		F.						vd	gf.		2					Alley.
Hart's-lane		W.F.	P.	G.				vd	gf.					4	1	
John's-place, Essex-street		F.						d	gf.	pf.						Alley.
Jubilee-place, Parliament-st	8	F.	P.					vd	gf.	pf.	35			2	2	P Alley
Lamb-gardens		F.						vd	gf.	pf.	5		2	1	1	G.
Lamb-place		F.			D.			vd	gf.	pf.						
Lamb-row		F.			D.			vd	gf.	pf.						
Lamb-street		F.			D.			vd	gf.	pf.						
Little Collingwood-street	42	F.						vd	gf.	pf.	12		2		2	Alley.
Little Manchester-street	W.	F.				C.							1	3	1	
Lisbon-street		F.	P.		D.			vd	gf.				1	1	3	
London-street, North-street	W	F.				C.		d	gf.				1		2	
Lucas-street		F.	P.					vd	gf.		27					
Manchester-buildings	9							vd	gf.				1	1		Alley.
Manchester-passage or place	5							d			18		1	1		
Middle-walk, George-yard		F.						d	gf.							
Mape-street		W.						d	gf.				1	1	1	
Mary's-row, Essex-street		F.						vd		pf.						Alley.
New York-street	W	F.	P.					vd	gf.		42		1	7	4	
North Conduit-street	W	F.	P.		D.	S.		d	gf.		45	1				
North-street					D.			d								
New-square, North-street		F.						vd	gf.	pf.			1			Alley.
New King's-street		F.			D.			vd					1	1		
Parliament-court	4	F.	P.		D.			vd	gf.		32				1	C.
Parliament-place	10	F.	P.		D.			d	gf.		31				1	Alley.
Parliament-street	21	F.	P.		D.			vd	gf.		33		2		2	
Pitt-street					D.			d	gf.	pf.	25		1	3	4	Alley.
Pleasant-place, North-st		F.						vd	gf.	pf.	11			5	2	Alley.
Pleasant-row, North-street		F.			D.			vd	gf.		10					C.
Pollard-row	W	F.	P.		D.		C.						2			
Pollard-street	W	F.			D.		C.	d							1	
Pott-street	W				D.			d	gf.		26			2		1
Primrose-street		F.						d	gf.		6		2			
Punderson-gardens	W	F.						vd	gf.	pf.	39			3	1	Alley.
Punderson-place, (Little)		F.						d				1	1			GAlley.
Queen-street		F.	P.		D.		C.							2		
Robert-street, Hart's-lane	W	F.						d	gf.			1	2	1		
Sale-street		F.			D.			d	gf.		9	1	1	4	1	

DISTRICT, No. 2.

Streets, Courts, and Alleys, &c.	Number of Houses.	Footpath F.	Footpath Paved P.	Granite Roadway G.	Street Drainage D.	Sewered S.	Streets Clean C.	Sts. dirty or very dsrty v vd.	Gutters full or overflowing gf.	Privies full or overflowing p f.	Nuisances, refer to figures.	Deaths from fever in 12 ms.	Dths frm other zymotic dis.	Cas of fev r attd by med offir.	Cases of zymotic dis in 12 ms	Courts C, Alleys A, Cul-de-sacs Cul, Private P, Gardens G.
Seabright-street	W	F.			D.				gf.							
Selby-street, East and West		F.			D.		C.		gf.				2			
Severne-place, Parliament-st		F.	P.		D.			d	gf.						1	
Smart's-gardens 3 Colt-lane								vd	gf.		8					GAlley.
Somerford-street, West		F.						vd	gf.			1	2			
Southampton-st, North-st	W	F.					C.					13			1	
Southampton-terrace do.	W	F.					C.									
South Conduit-street	W	F.	P.		D.		C.	d				2	3	3	4	
South-street	W	F.						d	gf.				1			
Squirres-street	W	F.						vd	gf.				1			
St. Andrew-street	W						C.					49		2	5	
Tapp-street		F.			D.			vd	gf.							
Teale-street	W	F.	P.		D.			vd	gf.				1			
Temple-street, North		F.						vd	gf.							Alley.
Tent-street	W	F.						d				7			1	
Thomas Passage and Walk		F.	P.		D.			vd	gf.			13		2	4	Alley.
Thomas-place								d	gf.							
Thomas-street, Beth.-grn-rd		F.			D.			d	gf.			1	9			
Thomas-pl., Beckford-street						S.		vd	gf.	pf.	15					Alley.
Three Colt Lane		F.			D.			vd	gf.			4		3	1	
Trafalgar Court, North-st					D.	½S		vd	gf.							Alley.
Trafalgar-place, ditto					D.			vd	gf.				1		6	Alley.
Violet-street, 3 Colt-lane		F.			D.			d								Alley.
Wellington-st., North-st		F.			D.			vd	gf.					1	1	
West-street, do do	W	F.						vd	gf.						1	Alley.
William-street							C.	d	gf.							
Wilmot-grove	W						C.	d	gf.			19		1		
Wilmot-street	W	F.			D.			d	gf.					1	5	
Wilmot-square		F.	P.		D.	S.	C.							1		
Winchester-st E of White-st	W	F.	P.					d	gf.							
Wolverley-st, Beth-gn-road	W	P.	P.				C.	d	gf.			47		3	4	Cul.
Wellington-street		F.	P.		D.	S.		d	gf.							
York-street		F.			D.			vd	gf.							Alley.

DISTRICT, No. 3.

The chief peculiarity of this district consists in its comparatively small number of courts and alleys, and the total absence of gardens. This part of the parish is about the oldest. The houses then built were chiefly to accommodate the weavers, and the practice followed was, to build a street of several stories, not, as is the present custom, to plant on the damp, undrained soil, two rooms on a ground floor. In this district, a very great number of the houses are built on a level from 18-inches to 2-feet below that of the path-way. Dust and dirt, therefore, readily become deposited in the houses, and there is much difficulty in cleansing them. In the summer season, moreover, they are very liable to have the mud washed into them. At all times they are very damp, and become sources of much disease to the inhabitants; rheumatism is extremely prevalent, and forms a large proportion of the cases of sickness. Over-crowding takes place to a great extent in this district. Many of the houses in Nelson-street, which have only four moderate sized rooms, have a family in each floor. The larger houses in Hare-street, Swan-street, and Bacon-street, are similarly overcrowded; sometimes as many as 14 persons sleep in one room. From six to nine is a common number. The chief occupants are mechanics and labourers, but principally weavers. Their earnings are very small and very precarious, and their habits are commonly intemperate. Many of the old streets which have granite road-ways, are in a most disgracefully broken-up state, rendering transit over them dangerous and disagreeable. The cleansing of the streets here seems to be utterly neglected. The complaints of the impossibility to have refuse removed by the contractor, are everywhere prevalent, loud, and deep. The same practice of scattering the slops, and all refuse on the streets is the rule. The same want of efficient drainage is manifest, and the same absence of sewerage is greatly to be deplored. Much poverty is apparent, and the causes of disease and death are to be found to an alarming extent. The water supply is conducted on the same outrageous principles of utter indifference to the welfare and comfort of the miserable tenants. There are *two* water closets in this district. One at the parsonage, another at the Green-gate, both of them drain into cesspools. Generally, there is one privy for every two houses, but in many instances there is only one for a much greater number. Some of them are very offensive.

This district contains the grave-yard attached to the parish church; 80,000 persons have been buried in it.

The railway has been, at once, a source of great benefit to this part of the parish, and of no slight evil. It has erased a great number of streets and alleys of the worst possible description, and thus effectually rid the parish of a cluster of houses containing a population ever paupers, ever sources of expense, through their sickness and mortality. But although it has thus removed a kind of property utterly unimprovable, it has produced considerable sources of disease in the filth and dirt which are permitted to accumulate around the bases of most of the arches. The great traffic, likewise, from the goods depôt, has broken up the streets and produced great uncleanness. On the whole, however, great benefit has arisen to this part of Bethnal-Green Parish by the passage of the railway through it. It is greatly to be deplored that a very great number of the houses which abut on it are in a most dilapidated, desolate, and wretched condition, and that no efficient steps are taken either to erase them, or to render them fit for habitation by human beings. In consequence of the numerous houses which have been taken down for the railway, and partly, perhaps, from the numerous officials employed by the Company, who require to reside near the terminus, a great demand has arisen for all kinds of houses, and of lodgings. I observed in all my travels through this district but two empty houses; these were two-roomed, and, doubtless, would speedily be occupied.

The same streets, which, 10 years ago, were considered the most unhealthy, and which were remarkable for their great mortality from epidemics, at the present time exhibit the same causes of disease, and a similar high mortality. No improvement, worthy of the name, has been effected, though the lamentable facts of the great prevalence of disease and high mortality have long been notorious.

The following illustrations are the records of my personal inspections of this district:—

GRANBY-ROW, ABBEY-STREET, 1.—This row is west, and a continuation, of Thomas-passage, described in District, No. 2. The houses are situated eighteen inches below the level of the roadway, and are therefore very damp. The drainage is most imperfect, and unworthy of the name. There are dust-heaps and garbage-collections near most of the houses, and reeking dung-heaps close by the windows. One stand-tap supplies every three or four houses. This row is in the most abominable state of dirt and filth that can well be imagined. The path is most unequal, full of puddles of mud and filth, and nearly impassable. The centre gutter or surface drain is full and most filthy. The miserable yards in front of these houses are abominably filthy; the privies are full and offensive. The yards themselves are covered with open surface drains and shallow pools, full of offensive and fœtid slimy mud. All kinds of slops and garbage are strewn everywhere on the surface. The houses are very wretched. This place was formerly called Botany Bay, as if to characterise a place where none but those fit for extrusion from society could reside. Certainly if the name was intended to convey an idea of a place altogether beyond the bounds of civilisation it was extremely appropriate. The dwellings of the wretched persons who live here are as dirty internally as they are externally.

DERBYSHIRE-ST., WEST, 2.—On this dirty street is thrown much garbage. The houses on the south side are two feet below the level of the road.

RAMSEY-ST, 3.—The houses on the east side are much below the level of the road. The British Schools are situated here.

WINCHESTER-PLACE, 4.—The yards at the back of the houses in this place, and between it and Chelsea-place, are in a *perfectly* beastly state. They are covered with dung, refuse, and garbage heaps. The soil emits a most offensive smell.

WINCHESTER CRESCENT, 5.—This is a very filthy court. The yards at the west side are bounded by a high and dead wall; those on the east side are excessively foul, in fact they are in a state resembling a pig-stye. The houses on both sides, are below the level of the pathway; 3s. and 4s. 6d. weekly are paid as rent. Some nine months ago the whole of the inhabitants of this court were ill of fever.

WOOD-ST., 6.—This street is in a very filthy condition. At the north-eastern end is a cow-yard, in which there is a very large accumulation of pasty dung, boarded-up. The place is excessively dirty, and smells most offensively. From 40 to 50 cows are usually kept here.

HARE-ST, 7.—This street is abominably dirty and foul; a condition which results from no imperfection of the street itself, as it is well paved and has a good roadway. The back yards of the houses here are in a most scandalous state. Let us take one as an example:—The back-yard of No. 79 is in a perfectly beastly state of filth; the privy is full, and smells most offensively. There is a large cess-pool in it, one part of which is only partially covered with boarding; the night-soil was lately removed from it, but the stench arising from it is still very great. In another part is a little puddle, or pond, of fœtid semi-putrescent mud. A pig-stye has lately been removed, but the organic remains common to such places, are mixed up with the earth, and form a pasty mass spread over part of the soil. The wife of the present occupier lately died of fever, and his child recovered with great difficulty. None of the inhabitants are well; three cases of fever and one death were clearly traceable to the abominable filthiness of this place.

HARE MARSH, 8.—On the north of the railway the footpaths are paved, and there is a granite roadway. Notwithstanding these favourable circumstances the street is abominally dirty and covered with mud and decaying garbage. Under the arch are accumulations of filth, but to the south of the railway the place is in a deplorably foul and desolate state. Four houses here present every mark of the extreme of dilapidation, decay, and wretched poverty; the back-yards are perfect pig-styes, covered with mud, filth, and nastiness. One tap supplies three houses with water.

ST. JOHN SRTEET, 9.—The arches of the railway, which run along the south side of this street, are converted into stables for the horses employed by the railway company. This street is very dirty. At the "Fighting Cock," which is at the east corner of the street, forming part of Hare-street, seven persons were attacked with cholera, during the epidemic, who all died within three days. The roadway of this street is broken up, and in a very bad state; it is also thickly populated Dr. Smith said nine years ago, "Malignant fever has been remarkably prevalent, and has stalked from house to house;" the railroad, however, has taken down one entire side of the street. Fever, however, is still common in this street, which is one of the most unhealthy in the district.

THREE COLT CORNER, &c., 10.—This place is very dirty, garbage lies on all parts of the roadway.

KNIGHTLY COURT, 11.—This court is in a very dilapidated state. In it there are two privies in a beastly state, full, and the contents flowing into the court. There is one dust reservoir. One stand-tap supplies the seven houses. The court at the further end of this court is quite unpaved, and in a nasty filthy state; two cases of severe typhus lately occurred here, one died. These wretched houses are let at 3s. 6d. per week.

PETLEY-ST., 12.—The roadway is broken up and full of holes, and more resembles the remains of an ancient Roman road, than a modern roadway.

FLEET-ST., 13.—This street is most abominably filthy, the gutters are full and partly cover the street with fœtid, black, slimy mud; garbage is frequently thrown over its surface; the houses are elevated, consisting of several flats, with different families in each; the ventilation of the rooms is most imperfect, and the smell from them most disagreeable. It will be observed that fever and the other epidemics are rife in this dirty place. Horse-ride in Fleet-street, is very filthy.

FLEET-ST. HILL, 14.—A great part of this place is most abominably filthy.

FIEFS-COURT, 15.—For the 10 houses there is one dust-heap at the end of the court, the ashes and refuse of which continually slide down from the heap, and choke up the drain in this court, and cause a pool of fluid filth to stagnate, and defile the place. The houses are two-roomed, and let at 2s. 6d. a week.

WILLIAM-ST., 16.—A very dirty gutter is in the centre of this street.

BLACKBIRD-ALLEY, 17.—The archway No. 29 has deposited around it garbage and refuse, and is beastly dirty.

COLLIER-COURT, LITTLE GEORGE-ST, 18.—The inhabitants of this little court take great pains and bestow much labour in attempting to keep it clean; but the loss of time and the labour necessary to keep it clean are greatly complained of. There is one privy, one tap, and one dust-bin common to the three houses, which are two-roomed. Rent 3s. a week.

GREAT GEORGE-ST., 19.—In this street is a yard, containing stables and cowsheds, which is very dirty, having much refuse on its surface.

WHITE'S-COURT, GREAT GEORGE-ST., 20.—In this court are several dust and garbage-heaps; one tap is common to six, and another, to two houses.

BUTLER'S-BUILDINGS, 21.—In this court, or alley, are eight, small, two-roomed houses, and two large houses with four or five rooms. There is one tap common to all, and one dust-heap; but there are eight privies, which are nearly full, and in a most filthy condition. The two larger houses are dark, close, and desolate-looking; three cases of fever occurred in them lately.

PULLEN'S-BUILDINGS, 22.—Two only of the six houses in this alley are in Bethnal-Green parish. There is one dust-bin in common, and one tub to supply water; but, for some reason unknown to the inhabitants, the supply has been cut off from them by the Water Company, and they are now compelled to get it as they best can, and "from anybody" who will give it to them.

ANCHOR-ST., 23.—This street has just undergone the (nominal) process of cleansing, and presents an excellent example of the manner in which this work is gone about; the semi-fluid, black, fœtid mud has been swept into the gutters, and chokes them up, a part being washed on to the foot-pavement; the slime still covers, in a tolerably thick layer, the surface of the street, and presents the most disgusting proofs of the abundance of vegetable and animal remains, which are mixed up and incorporated with the mud; the odour arising from this street is most offensive.

At the foot of York-street, and leading from this street, is the archway referred to in my Lecture (p. 25). This archway extends for a very considerable distance, having been greatly prolonged by the additions lately made to the terminus. This passage is partly covered over with wooden cross-beams, but at the extremity two stone arches are placed at right angles to each other. The parish of Bethnal-green has a right of way here, which it would not yield to the Railway Company; the passage therefore remains. It is nearly perfectly dark, and is made use of by the public to deposit every kind of excremental refuse, garbage, and filth; animal and vegetable remains of all kinds are thrown there in every stage of decomposition. Last time I visited this horrid place I passed through it, but now it is so disgusting that I would not (accustomed even as I have been to every kind of offensive nuisance) advance beyond the threshold of it; the odour arising from this place is most offensive;—it is absolutely necessary that this passage be shut up; in its present state it constitutes a most disgusting and abominable nuisance, alike destructive to health and offensive to every feeling of delicacy.

LITTLE YORK-ST., 24.—This street is in the same condition as Anchor-street, equally filthy and abominable, and disgraceful to the authorities.

LITTLE ANCHOR-ST., 25.—This street is in a similar condition to the foregoing, with the exception that mud-heaps are piled on it every few yards; in it there is a large yard in a most filthy state; stabling-sheds for carts cover the ground.

CLUB-ROW, 26.—This street is in a perfectly beastly condition, and resembles the surface of a pig-stye more than a roadway made for the accommodation and traffic of civilized beings; on it are scattered heaps of garbage and collections of mud. The roadway itself is much broken up, so that to journey over it in any vehicle produces the most painful and distressing jolting.

BACON-ST., 27.—This street is very filthy; garbage is strown on the surface, and mud-heaps occur every few yards; in it there is a cow-yard, with the usual collection of putrescent animal and vegetable refuse. This street has long possessed a disgraceful notoriety for its dirty state, and the prevalence of disease in it.

SWAN-ST., 28.—This street is an abomination, its condition utterly disgraceful, and greatly to be reprehended. The effects of such a condition of things are manifested in the fact that the parochial medical officer receives more orders for attendance upon the sick here than he does for any other place in his district.

Swan-street is densely crowded, and celebrated for its unhealthiness and its high mortality.

SWAN-COURT, 29.—This court, like the street from which it derives its name, is abominably filthy; there are three open privies belonging to it, they are full, and most disgusting; there are, likewise, two more privies situated in the court, but they do not belong to it. Dust-heaps, ordure, and garbage are scattered about, as are also shallow pools of liquid fœtid filth. The houses convey the impression of desolation; the surface, that of great moral debasement and degradation among the occupants; the whole locality, that of wretchedness and misery, and disease. The medical officer at one time attended here six cases of fever, being all the occupants of one room; they all lay in one bed. He also attended in another house, at the same time, three cases of small-pox, two of which died, and a case of jaundice. All this disease was mainly attributable to the impure atmosphere.

LITTLE BACON-ST., 30.—This street is in an equally beastly condition with Club-row (vide 26), the description of which perfectly applies to it.

BUSBY-SQUARE, 31.—This square is perfectly dirty; the houses are two feet below the level of the court-yard; there are two privies in it, which are full, and one dust and garbage-heap; there is likewise one tap for the supply of water.

BUSBY-COURT, 32.—The houses here are two feet below the level of the yard, and are very damp. One tap supplies five houses; there is a privy to each house, which is emptied once a year. The inhabitants think this an unexampled instance of cleanliness, and consider " they would be very well off, if things were always as comfortably managed."

GRANBY-ROW, JAMES-ST., 33.—The houses here are below the level of the footpath, which is *clean*—a most unusual occurrence. In front of these houses is an open space, consisting of the back yards of the adjoining houses; in this space are eight open privies.—This description contrasts most favourably with that of Dr. Southwood Smith, published nine years ago.

EDWARD-ST., 34.—To these houses there are three privies attached; one tap, and one dust and garbage-heap; the houses are two-roomed, and rented at 3s. 6d. per week.

DISTRICT, No. 3.

Streets, Courts, and Alleys, &c.	Number of Houses	Footpath F.	Footpath Paved P.	Granite Roadway G.	Street Drainage D.	Sewerage S.	Street Clean C.	Sts. dirty or very dirty vd.	Gutters full or ovrflowing gf.	Privies full or overflowing pf.	Nuisances refer to figures	Deaths from fever in 12 ms.	Dths frm other zymotic dis.	Cass of f'r attd by med offic.	C's of zymotic dis in 12 ms.	Courts C, Alleys A, Cul-desacs Cul, Private P, Gardens G.
Abbey-street		F.	P.		D.		C.	d				2				
Anchor-street		F.	P.	G.	D.			d	gf.		23	1	4		3	
Anchor-court	1				D.			d								C.
Anglesea-street		F.		G.				vd	gf.			3				
Bacon-street		F.	P.	G.	D.	S.		vd	gf.		27	1	7	5	4	
Beth-gn-rd., s.w of White-st		F.	P.	G.				vd	gf.			5	5			
Blackbird-alley		F.	P.	G.	D.			vd	gf.	pf.	17				1	Alley.
Brick-lane, in this parish		F.	P.	G.				vd	gf.			3			3	
Busby-court	3		P.					vd		pf.	32					C.
Busby-square	7							vd	gf.	pf.	31	1				C.
Busby-street		F.						vd	gf.			4				
Butler's-blds, Gt. George-st	10	F.	P.		D.			d		pf.	21	1	1	2		Alley.
Carlisle-street		F.						vd	gf.			3				
Carter-st., Brick-lane		F.	P.	G.	D.	S.	C.						1	1	3	
Carter-st., Weaver-st		F.	P.	G.	D.	S.		d	gf.			1				
Charles-street, Petley-st		F.	P.		D.			vd	gf.			2				
Cheshire-st., W. of White-st		F.						vd	gf.			1	2			
Church-row		F.	P.		D.			vd	gf.				1	6	4	
Church-st. S. Bethnal-gn-rd		F.	P.		D.								1		2	
Clarence-st., Anglesea-st		F.	P.				C.									
Club-row		F.	P.	G.	D.	S.		vd	gf.		26					
Collier-ct., Little George-st	3	F.	P.		D.		C.				18					Alley.
Derbyshire-street		F.	P.		D.			vd	gf.	pf.	2		5		2	Alley.
Edward-court	6	F.	P.		D.	S.		vd	gf.							Alley.
Edward-street		F.	P.		D.	S.		d	gf.	pf.	34	1	2	4	5	
Farthing-hill, in this parish		F.	P.		D.			vd					1	2		Alley.
Fief's-court, Fleet-street	10	F.			D.			d	gf.		15			1	3	
Fleet-street			P.	G.	D.			vd	gf.		13	1	10	5	6	
Fleet-street-hill		F.	P.	G.				vd	gf.		14			1	7	
Fuller-street		F.	P.					d	gf.			2		2	1	
Granby-row, Abbey-street		F.		G.	D.			vd	gf.	pf.	1		2			Alley.
Granby-row, James-st		F.	P.		D.	S.	C.		gf.		33			2	4	
Granby-street		F.	P.		D.	S.		d	gf.							
Granby-terrace, James-st		F.			D.			d								
Gt. George-st		F.	P.	G.	D.			d	gf.		19					
Gt. Manchester-st		F.						d	gf.			2				
Gt. York-st., in this parish		F.	P.	G.				vd	gf.							
Hare-court	4	F.	P.		D.			d								Alley.
Hare Marsh		F.	P.	G.	D.	S.		vd	gf.	pf.	8			2	2	Cul.
Hare-street		F.	P.	G.	D.			vd	gf.	pf.	7		6	6	5	

DISTRICT, No. 3.

Streets, Courts, and Alleys, &c.	Number of Houses.	Footpath F.	Footpath Paved P.	Granite Roadway G.	Street Drainage D.	Sewerage S.	Streets Clean C.	Sts. dirty or very dty d. vd.	Gutters full or overflowing gf.	Privies full or overflowing pf.	Nuisances refer to figures.	Dths from fvr in 12 months.	Dths from other zymotic dis.	Cases of fvr attd by med offrr.	Cs of othr zymtic dis in 12 ms	Courts C, Alleys A, Cul-de-sacs Cul. Private P. Gardens G.
Hereford-buildings	..	F	P	..	..	..	C	..	..	..	..	..	1	..	..	C.
Hereford-street	..	F	..	..	..	..	..	vd	gf.	..	..	1	..	..	..	..
Horse Ride, Fleet-st	8	..	..	..	..	..	..	vd	gf.	..	..	1	..	..	..	Alley
James-st., Church-st	..	F	P	..	..	..	..	vd	gf.	..	..	1	2	1	2	..
Knightly-ct., Three-colt-cur	7	..	P	..	D	..	..	vd	..	pf.	11	1	..	1	..	C.
Little-Anchor-street	..	F	P	..	D	..	..	vd	gf.	..	25	..	..	..	..	..
Little Bacon-st	..	F	P	G.	D	..	..	vd	gf.	..	30	..	..	..	..	..
Little-York-street	..	F	P	G.	..	..	..	vd	gf.	..	24	1	..	1	2	..
Molly's-alley, Fleet-st	..	F	..	..	..	..	..	..	..	..	..	..	..	..	..	..
New Church-st lte Ram-ally	..	F	P	G.	D	S	..	d	gf.	..	..	..	..	..	..	..
New King-st., James-st	..	F	..	..	..	S	..	vd	gf.	..	..	..	1	2	1	..
Nottingham-street	..	F	P	..	D	S	..	..	..	..	..	1	2	1	..	..
Oakey-street	..	F	P	..	D	..	..	vd	gf.	..	..	..	2	..	..	..
Patience-street	..	F	P	G.	..	..	..	vd	gf.	..	..	..	1	..	..	..
Petley-street	..	F	P	..	D	..	..	d	gf.	..	12	..	2	..	4	..
Pullen's-blds., Patience-st	2	F	P	..	D	..	..	..	..	..	22	..	..	..	..	Alley.
Ramsey-street	..	F	..	..	D	..	..	d	gf.	..	3	..	..	..	..	..
St. John-street	..	F	P	G.	D	..	..	vd	gf.	..	9	2	3	4	4	..
Sale-st., West of White-st.	..	F	..	..	D	..	..	d	gf.	..	..	..	..	..	..	..
Scalter-street	..	F	P	G.	..	..	..	vd	gf.	..	..	..	3	1	2	..
Short-street, Patience-street	..	F	P	G.	..	..	..	vd	gf.	..	..	..	..	..	..	..
Spicer-st., in this parish	..	F	P	..	D	S	..	vd	gf.	..	..	1	..	..	..	..
Stephen's-bldngs., Petley-st	..	F	P	..	D	..	..	vd	gf.	..	..	..	1	..	..	Alley.
Swan-st	..	F	P	G.	..	..	..	vd	gf.	pf.	28	..	1	2	6	..
Swan-court	7	..	..	G.	D	..	..	vd	gf.	..	29	..	2	6	4	Alley.
Tavistock-street	14	..	..	..	..	..	..	vd	gf.	..	..	..	2	2	..	..
Thomas-st., Brick-lane	..	F	P	..	D	S	..	vd	gf.	..	..	1	..	2	7	..
Three-Colt-Corner, Hare-st	..	F	P	G.	D	S	..	vd	gf.	..	10	..	..	2	1	..
Weaver-street	..	F	P	G.	D	S	..	vd	gf.	..	..	..	3	2	1	..
Wellington-street	..	F	P	..	D	S	..	d	gf.	..	..	..	2	..	..	..
West Selby-street	..	..	..	..	..	..	C	..	..	..	..	..	..	..	..	..
Wheeler-st., in this parish	..	F	..	G	..	..	..	vd	gf.	..	..	..	..	..	..	..
Whites-ct., Gt. George-st.	..	F	P	..	D	..	C	d	..	..	20	..	1	..	..	Alley.
White-street	..	F	P	..	..	..	..	d	gf.	..	..	..	8	..	1	..
William-st., late Blkbird-aly	..	F	P	G.	D	..	..	vd	gf.	..	16	1	2	..	..	..
Winchester-place	..	..	..	..	..	..	..	vd	..	pf.	4	..	..	..	..	C.
Winchester-street	..	F	P	..	..	..	..	d	gf.	..	..	1	1	1	1	..
Winchester or Reform Csnt	..	F	P	..	..	..	..	d	gf.	pf.	5	..	..	1	1	C,
Woods Close	..	F	P	..	D	..	..	d	gf.	..	..	..	..	..	..	..
Wood-street	..	F	P	..	D	..	..	vd	gf.	..	6	..	..	..	..	..

DISTRICT, No. 4.

This district exceeds all those which have gone before it in filth, disease, mortality, poverty, and wretchedness; it abounds with the most foul courts, and is characterised by the prevalence of the greatest nuisances, and perennial foulness. Unlike the last district, there are several gardens in it resembling those already described, but infinitely surpassing them in everything degrading to our civilization. For many years this district has been notorious as the hot-bed of epidemics. This is easily explained, when the foulness of the streets, the dense crowding in some parts, and the nearly total absence of drainage and house-cleansing, are considered. The drainage, in fact, is characteristic of primitive barbarism; the drains are very near the surface, and some of the houses are built over them; the streets are perpetually covered with the most offensive fœtid mud; the population is very dense, as many as 30 persons residing in a single house—57 houses had a population of 580 persons. In about half a mile square of these houses and streets 30,000 persons are congregated; the houses are generally of the worst class, and four-roomed, but great numbers resemble, in many respects, those in the worst parts of the Old Town of Edinburgh—a class of houses common to the French, and which they were the cause of introducing into both places. The houses built by the French refugees are all several storied, and have large rooms on each floor, with a common staircase; the houses are, without exception, let out in rooms; each room contains a family, with a bed common to all; generally it is a work-room as well as a dwelling-room. Ventilation in these rooms is in the most defective state; the atmosphere is most oppressive, and loaded with unhealthy emanations; it is a common practice to retain the fœcal remains in the rooms, in order to avoid exposure, and the perfect nastiness of, the common privies. The parochial medical officer has not seen, and does not know of, one water-closet in the whole district. All the tenements in Greengate-gardens are unfit for human habitation; they are much under the level of the neighbouring road, and are very damp; they smell most offensively. There are great numbers of low public-houses and beer-shops in this district; all these are crowded with lodgers, and thus become great nuisances, and sources of disease and immorality. Since several streets have been pulled down by the Railway Company, there has been much overcrowding; so much so, that not a habitation or lodging can be had in the neighbourhood, and some persons are, even now, in opposition to the law, residing in cellars, because they can find no place else to reside. The poor inhabitants generally prefer any kind of abode to the workhouse. The occupations of the inhabitants are chiefly weaving and shoe-making; hawkers, toy-makers, and cabinet-makers, abound here, and the women wind silk and cotton. Those small manufactures which are carried on here are chiefly prepared in the prospect of being sold to the ready-money shops, or on speculation. The earnings of the population of this district are very low and precarious, their habits most irregular, and generally intemperate—to-day an unexpected " stroke of luck" supplies them with means to indulge their appetites with dainties and abundance—tomorrow sees them deprived of the most inferior kinds of sustenance. No pru- or forethought prevents them from living on the best, when they can, or restrains their ill-regulated appetites. Their common food consists of potatoes and bread, and butcher's meat of a very inferior quality. Numerous chandlers' shops are in the habit of supplying this inferior kind of food, and of receiving goods as pledges for its payment; these pledges are sold at the end of a month, if unredeemed. Moral debasement and physical decay, naturally enough, accompany the utter defiance of all the laws of health, and the complete disregard of all the characteristics of civilization. Such a population always supply our courts with criminals, our gaols with convicts, our charities with paupers, and our hospitals with the sick and diseased; and impoverish the honest, labouring poor, by the heavy poor-rates to which they give rise.

WILLOW-WALK, 1.—There is one stand-tap to four houses in this court, but there is no receptacle for refuse; there is a cow-shed in it. The houses are two-roomed, and let at 3s. a week. None of the inhabitants earn 10s. a week.

GREENGATE-GARDENS, 2, 3.—These gardens are divided into "three walks;" the first, the middle, and third. The first contains eight houses, which are in a most wretched condition, planted on the clay, and without drainage of any kind. One of them has a cesspool, which is not emptied more than once in three years; the others have three privies, which are full, and most disgustingly offensive. The houses contain two rooms on the ground floor, and are let at 3s. 6d. per week. The average earnings of the inhabitants are 6s. per week. One water-tap is common to five houses; three houses are without any water supply, and the occupants require to obtain it at the "Green-Gate" public-house. In the middle walk the greatest dirtiness and filthiness prevail; all the privies are full, and have not been emptied for at least four years; many are overflowing, and the contents spread over the yard; all kinds of refuse and garbage are thrown in front of the houses, for want of dust-bins; holes are dug in the earth to receive the slops; collections of dung and manure abound in some places. 2s. 6d. a week are paid for these houses, and the average earnings are 6s. per week. The third walk is still more filthy than the rest; excrements are scattered about, all the privies are full and overflowing, and the soil desiccating in the sun. One stand-pipe, beside a dung-heap, is the only means by which 30 houses are supplied with water; of course quarrels for precedence and to ensure a supply are common. The whole of these gardens are in a condition alike disgusting and disgraceful. Being private property, they are never cleansed by the parish, but are left in a perpetual state of dirt and nastiness; they are excessively damp, and most noisome. The tenements, as has been remarked, are unfit for human habitation; disease is always common here; some of the worst cases of typhus fever were removed from this locality to the workhouse.

STROUT-PLACE, 4.—This place is always very dirty, from cattle going and returning to a cow-shed, the smell from which is frequently very offensive, and is much complained of.

CRESCENT-PLACE, 5.—One pump in the centre of the crescent, communicating with a sunk tank supplied from the main, supplies all the 25 houses.

SOMERSET-BUILDINGS, 6.—The drainage is imperfect, the drains being stopped. A tap supplies every two houses, which are two and three-roomed.

CRABTREE-ROW, 7.—The privies at the back of Somerset-buildings abut on the street, and are only separated by a boarding; the surface drainage flows into street-gutter, and stagnates there, and the soil from the privies oozes into the main road. At the south-end of these buildings all kinds of garbage, putrefying remains of fish, and every kind of refuse, are deposited by the public, to the great annoyance and injury of the occupants. Opposite to this row there is a very large triangular open space, which has been made by the removal of numerous gardens and houses similar to those described under the head of Greengate-gardens—a removal at once beneficial to the neighbourhood and the occupants, as it is the only open space in this densely-populated district. But although the houses have been swept from the ground, the holes attached to the privies and cesspools were only partially filled up; a considerable quantity of night-soil, therefore, remains mixed up with the ground and refuse on the surface; in addition, being waste ground, and quite open, it is largely made use of to deposit all kinds of dirt, garbage, and excrementitious matter, which are allowed to dry in the sun. After rain (which stagnates, on account of the level), and in warm weather, a very offensive odour arises from this place; it is greatly complained of in the neighbourhood as a resort for all the reprobate characters in the vicinity on Sundays, who there gamble, fight, and indulge in all kinds of indecencies and immoralities. The passers-by on Sundays are always sure to be subjected to outrage in their feelings, and often in their persons. The enclosing of the space would be considered "a great blessing."

TRAFALGAR-PLACE, NICHOLS-ROW, 9.—In this street the privy and the water-barrel are in juxta-position. Water is laid on to each house. A quantity of refuse of every description is piled against the wall in front; the surface-drains are choked up, and the place, consequently, very dirty.

AUSTIN-ST., 10.—This street is one of the filthiest in the metropolis, and is contiguous to Shoreditch Church-yard. There is a new cow-yard in it, which is very clean.

OLD CASTLE-ST., 11.—Garbage is thrown all about the street, there to decompose.

OLD CASTLE-COURT, 12.—This court is abominably filthy; it has never been cleaned in 16 or 17 months; the yard and gutters are full of fœtid fluid, arising from the drainage of collections of garbage and foul heaps, and from the inundations of the overflowing privies. 5s. 9d are paid for these dilapidated three-roomed houses. Ten houses, containing 28 families, have two stand-pipes in the yard to supply them with water. The inhabitants complained loudly, deeply and bitterly, of the state of their court, and would willingly contribute 4d. per week for relief.

SWEET APPLE-COURT, 13.—The gutter in the centre of this court was very filthy; garbage was strewn about, the privies were quite full and dilapidated. Each house has water supplied to it, but by a cock let through the wall; and as the house is parcelled out, whenever the person who inhabits the first floor is from home, and the door therefore locked, no one can procure water. This may happen when the water is on, and a great difficulty in obtaining it may thence arise. From the dripping of the water-pipe the place had become damp, and on opening the door, a horrid odour of nastiness, like putrid paste, was found to pervade the room.

BAKER'S-COURT, VIRGINIA-ROW, 14.—Pig-styes and donkeys are here; they create an offensive nuisance.

MINING'S-PLACE, MOUNT-ST., 15.—There is no dust-bin, but there are piles of refuse. There are two privies to the eight houses; they are overflowing, and most filthy. A large cesspool, covered by a board, is in the centre of this little court. Excrements are strewn about. There is no supply of water for these eight houses.

COLLINGWOOD-PLACE, 16.—In one of the houses in this place, formerly No. 13, Mount, which is two-roomed, about 8 feet high, and 8 by 9½ feet in length and breadth, and 4 feet below the level of the street, I found a family of six persons, who all slept in one (the front room), the other being very damp. The man's name was Johnston. His wife was dangerously ill of typhoid erysipelas on the miserable bed, on which the whole family usually slept. The rest of the family therefore had to sleep on the bare boards, in the same room with the sufferer, thus further defiling the impure atmosphere of this dark and damp abode of helpless poverty. 1s. 6d. a week was the rent; yet the husband's peculiar trade failing him, he had, for a considerable time, been unable to earn more than 1s. a week; they were, therefore, all starving. Nevertheless, in the belief that he would get work next week, he would not consent to place himself and his four children in the workhouse, the only terms upon which, even in her most dangerous condition, his wife could be admitted into the workhouse. Nine years ago, Dr. Smith recorded the fact, that out of seven houses in this court, fever had prevailed in five, and that in No. 6, six persons had been attacked. Here, then, nine years after it has been put on record that this place is a disgraceful nuisance—that it is a den of pestilence—do we still find all the elements of the disease rank and rife—still do we find the connection between filth and fever made apparent by the suffering of the unhappy occupants. The privies attached to this place were full and most offensive. There was no dust-bin, but heaps of garbage and refuse were scattered about. In this place ten houses have one water-tap; two privies are common to seven houses; they were full and most disgusting. The houses, as already mentioned, are two-roomed; they are let at 2s. 6d. a week. Where two families reside in one house, 3s. is the rent. There are thirteen families in the ten houses.

LITTLE COLLINGWOOD-ST., 17.—There are collections of mud and filth here. One tap supplies two houses.

Nelson-st., 18.—In this street is a cow-yard; there are also dung-heaps. The privies are also full and offensive.

Broadway, Austin-st., 20.—Collections of garbage are on the streets, and all kinds of decomposing vegetable refuse.

Boundary-st., 21.—In this street there are most offensive smells from tripe-boiling, from collections of old bones from marine-store shops, and from tallow-melting, carried on in the adjoining parish of Shoreditch.

Half Nichol-st., 22.—On the surface of this street were bountifully strewn all kinds of dust, dirt, refuse, and garbage. It is not cleansed more than once in three weeks or a month; and though cleansed (nominally) only last week, it was as filthy and dirty as if apparently it had not been cleansed for months. This state of very many of the streets arises not only from the extreme want of accommodation for storing refuse till the dustman shall remove it, but from the dust contractor utterly neglecting to remove it. The inhabitants, therefore, in order to get rid of all their refuse, solid as well as fluid, are compelled to throw it on the streets, there to putrefy and be mixed up with the mud. In consequence of the free exposure of the animal and vegetable remains in a pasty state to the sun, the muddy compost becomes most offensive to the smell, and a constant cause of disease and death to the inhabitants. Invariably, wherever such filthy streets are found, so likewise are fever and the other zymotic diseases. Loud complaints were made to me that the only way to get rid of the refuse was to throw it on the streets, as the dustmen would not take it away unless paid for so doing. The inhabitants of this street complained bitterly that "the people in it never died a natural death, but were murdered by the fever." In the back yards of No. 21 in this street the soakage from the neighbouring privies had permeated through the wall, infiltrated it, and spread itself over the yard, where the offensive fœtid soil was covered over, and as it were dammed up by collections of dust, cinders, and refuse. The poor-rate collector complained of this place as a great nuisance.

Short-st., &c., 23.—On this street are collections of garbage, &c.

Nichol's-row, 24.—A cellar here serves at once for a dust-bin and a privy. The yards were filthy, and filled with refuse.

Mead-st., 25.—In this street alone, in the whole district, was there a good fall of water in the gutters. Garbage and refuse of all kinds were liberally strewn on the street. The gully-holes emitted the most offensive odours. The privies in this street are generally full and overflowing.

Turville-st., 26.—On this street, likewise, garbage and refuse are abundantly distributed; the street itself is most dirty.

Turville-buildings, 27.—Collections of dust, dirt, and refuse and vegetable remains are here. The inhabitants stated that, on account of the landlord being in debt to the water-company, ten houses were deprived of their supply of water. Eight houses are at present without any supply. Two privies are common to three houses, and one privy is common to seven houses; they are all nasty, and horribly offensive.

George-terrace, Turville-st., 28.—There is one dust-heap, and one stand-pipe to supply water, common to five houses. The cock is cut off, and when the water comes on it continues to run and deluge the place.

Thomas-place, Old Nichol-st, 30.—The privies are close to the houses, and the smell is offensive.

Shepherd's-court, Old Nichol-st., 31.—This court is excessively dirty, and foul; the privies are confined and dirty; excrements are scattered abroad.

Maidstone-place, Old Nichol-st., 32.—There is a quantity of refuse collected here, and the place is very wet.

Devonshire-place, Old Nichol-st., 33.—One tap in a small court out of this place supplies the nine houses. In this court there is a refuse-heap.

New Nichol-st., 34.—The roadway is in a most dilapidated condition and most disgusting, from the surface being covered with refuse, garbage, mud, &c.

New Court, New Nichol-st., 35.—This is a narrow confined court, supplied with one dust-bin, and a privy, for every two houses. The water runs from a stand-tap into a long, narrow, open tank, which is next to the privy. There is also another open privy common to three houses, and opposite to it a barrel containing water.

Shacklewell-st., 36.—This is a narrow street containing a great number of inhabitants. Near to the entrance of this street, and within a yard, there is a considerable collection of dung, &c. There are twenty-six houses at the further end of this street; at the south-west end one tap is common to four houses; at the north side, in consequence of a quarrel between the landlords and the water company, eleven houses have been deprived of their supply of water. The back yards to these houses are 2½ feet deep by the frontage. In them are the privies, most of the privies are full and offensive. These houses are situated within a few feet south of Gibraltar Chapel grave-yard. On entering No. 23 the smell was most offensive, and was compared to that from a close confined vault in which the dead had long been retained. It seemed to me, however, to arise from some foul drain below the floor of the house. Be that as it may, decomposition takes place very rapidly in this street; meat becomes speedily tainted, and leather becomes covered with a green mould, even in one night. 3s. 6d. and 4s. a week are paid for these two-roomed houses. 12s. appears to be the extreme of the weekly earnings of the inhabitants; it was stated that not one earned 14s. a week. Sir James Tyrrell is the ground landlord of this street. Since the property has come into his possession no remedies have been applied to the discreditable condition of things which exists here, and has continued so long as to be a bye-word and a reproach.

Rose-st., 37.—A slaughter-house here is complained of as a great nuisance; there is likewise a stable with collections of dung.

Turk-st., 38.—This street presents another instance of the abominable nuisances which exist in London. A nightman has here formed a yard, where he has piled mountains of filth, dust, dirt, and ashes, mixed with decaying animal and vegetable remains and manure of all kinds. These are classified into separate little hills, and are piled as high as the houses, and cover a very large space of ground. The continual additions which are daily made to this enormous accumulation, and the sifting and the sorting of it, cause the loose particles on the surface to be wafted by each wind over the surrounding neighbourhood, to be deposited on the streets and in the houses, and to defile the air breathed by the inhabitants. This enormous depository of garbage and manure serves as a source whence to supply the neighbouring counties. From twenty-five miles round do the farmers send their carts to this yard to obtain that manure which, while on their fields, it serves to enrich the soil, in the midst of this dense poor and squalid population sows the seed of disease and death, and thus further impoverishes the wretched poor.

ROSE-PLACE, TURK-ST, 39.—This is a filthy court; a collection of dust is piled against a wall. The ground is most dirty, and covered with fœtid mud, which flows into a large hole or old cesspool, covered by a piece of board. No water is supplied to this den of nastiness. 2s. 3d. a week are paid as rent.

ALBION-PLACE, 40.—This place is very dirty; there is a dust and dirt heap; one stand-tap supplies seven houses. The gardens at the back of Turk-street are disgracefully filthy. 3s. 6d. a week are paid for the two-roomed houses in this court. The occupier of the one I inquired at has not earned 4s. a week for the last five months.

PROVIDENCE-PLACE, DUKE-ST., 41.—One privy, one tap, and one dust-heap are common to the eight houses.

PRINCES-COURT, VIRGINIA-ROW, 42.—This court is very dirty, owing to the insufficient drainage into Princes-place. When the surface-drain is stopped up (which frequently happens), and more especially when heavy rains fall, the six north-western houses are flooded with fœtid water, to a depth of four or five inches. The back yards of the houses in this court are not more than one yard square, excluding a privy. The six houses referred to, and two in Princes-place, are supplied with water from a stand-tap at one end of the court; the other fourteen houses are supplied from another tap at the other end. 2s. 6d. a week are paid for these two-roomed houses, the inhabitants of which earn 3s., 10s., or 12s. a week.

HEPWORTH-PLACE, FOUNTAIN-ALLEY, 43.—This court is in a most disgraceful and disgusting condition. It is below the level of the alley which leads to it; there is no drainage whatever. The fœtid fluid which *ever* covers its surface (receiving the soakage of the dust-heaps in the centre, and dissolving the vegetable and animal refuse lying about), whenever the rain falls, pours itself into the houses on the northern side, and inudates them. The privies closely attached to the back walls, permit their contents to infiltrate, and soak through, the walls of the houses, and to defile the lower rooms. One tap in the centre of the court is common to the fifteen houses of two rooms, of which the court is made up. 3s. a week are paid for the houses, and the inhabitants earn, on an average, from 12s. to 15s. a week.

PIERCES-PLACE, FOUNTAIN-ALLEY, 44.—This court is in a very filthy dirty state, and is covered with water. When the weather becomes wet, the houses are inundated with fœtid filth. There is a stable at the end; manure is kept there. There is one tap to supply water, one or two collections of dust and garbage, and a privy, in a most beastly state, pouring its contents upon the surface of the dirty yard.

THOMAS-PLACE, OLD NICHOL-ST., 45.—In this place there is a large collection of decomposing fœtid manure, and pultaceous refuse; it remains for a month before it is removed, again to be replaced.

SEVEN-STEP-COURT, CRABTREE-ROW, 46.—The four houses in this court, (like an immense number of the houses of the poor in this district), are unfit habitations for human beings. There is a putrid pool in the centre of the court, owing to the drain being choked up. The court is beastly dirty; there are dust heaps, one stand-tap, and one full and offensive privy in it.

WEATHERHEAD-GARDENS, 47.—The houses in these filthy gardens are in a most dilapidated condition; they have two rooms on the ground floor. The gardens, as they are termed, are considerably below the level of Crabtree-row; there is no drainage whatever. Collections of dust and garbage are near every dwelling-house; and the privies, though lately emptied, are very filthy; the whole place is very damp and excessively dirty, and conveys the impression of the utter absence of every social comfort. The entrance from Austin-street, called Hole-in-the-Wall, is abominably filthy. These gardens, and their approaches, like the other gardens in this parish, in wet weather are in the dirtiest state possible. Their dirty condition and the dilapidated dwellings correspond well with the character of the occupants, who are said to be thieves, gamblers, smashers, and vagabonds. 2s. 6d. a week are paid as rent; one stand-tap supplies twenty-two houses.

WELLS-COURT, CLARENCE-PLACE, 48.—This court is very filthy; there is one tap in it. Some dust-heaps, and a great stench from a dung-heap, and from the manure in the neighbouring dairy are observable.

STROUT-PLACE, 49.—Three of the houses, which are two-roomed, lead into Smith's-place; these have two common privies, and, as usual, they are full; dust-heaps and garbage are attached to each house. To these houses and to

SMITH'S-PLACE, &c., 50.—Eighteen two-roomed houses in this place, there is one stand-tap, with a small wooden tank to supply water; the tank itself was uncovered, and received, besides the impurities deposited from the atmosphere, the remains of fish and other refuse. Whenever the dust and garbage heaps, common to each house, are being removed, or receive additions, some of those particles which are suspended in the air unavoidably fall into the open tank. It is unnecessary here to speak of the deterioration of the water from the absorption of foul air, from privies, &c. In another court, in this place, four similar houses have a gutter in the centre of the court, full of fœtid refuse, a heap of dust, ashes, and garbage, and a dirty offensive privy. There is another court, in this place, containing eight houses; here there is a large collection of ashes and garbage, and a stagnant fœtid pool, arising from imperfect drainage. There is a stand-tap common to each two houses; but from there being no cock, when the water comes on, the place is flooded, and the refuse, mixed up into a paste, is spread over the surface of the yard, there to desiccate, and produce fever. The privies, here, are full and offensive; the houses themselves are so damp as to be uninhabitable on the ground-floor; two of the houses are two feet below the level of the court, so that when the water comes on, or after heavy rains, the floors of the lower rooms are inundated. It need scarcely be added that rheumatism and fever are common.

SMITH'S-BUILDINGS, 51.—There is a stable here, and of course dung-heaps, &c.

GIBRALTAR-WALK, 52.—Upon this street refuse and garbage are continually being thrown. All the slops of this, and a majority, I might almost say the whole, of the houses of this district, are thrown upon the streets; these remain on the surface, and become thoroughly incorporated with the mud, forming a thick, semi-pultaceous black fœtid mass. When the streets are cleansed, this matter is swept with brushes into the centre of the street, to remain in a heap till the cart shall come, into which it is to be thrown. As these streets are very imperfectly paved, a very considerable quantity of this putrid refuse still remains on the surface, and in the hollows between the boulder-stones. The first shower of rain washes this mud up, and renders the streets as filthy as if they had not been cleansed for months. The odour of these streets is *always* most offensive and disgusting. Near the southern end of this filthy walk are two gully-holes, which constantly emit the most abominable stenches, and give rise to fever in their neighbourhood.

BRENAN'S-PLACE, GIBRALTAR-WALK, 53.—The whole place is very filthy; excrements are strewn over the surface; there is no water laid on.

NORTON'S-GARDENS, GIBRALTAR-WALK, 54.—The drainage here is very insufficient, even though there is a sewer but a few yards from it; the place is very damp, and the soil dirty; there are no back yards to the houses; the privies are emptied about once a year, and are usually full and offensive. One open wooden tank in a state of decay, and covered with green mould, supplies these six houses, and six others situated in front, with water. The rent is 3s. 6d. a week; the average earnings of the occupants are 10s.

GIBRALTAR-PLACE, 55.—This place is gravelled in front, and has a good fall, so as always to be clean; the chapel and Sunday schools and a large burying-ground are here.

GIBRALTAR-GARDENS, 56.—The yards in front of these houses are partly very filthy; to the seventeen houses there is but one stand-tap.

THOROLD-SQ., 57.—This is a very filthy but open square of twenty-two dilapidated houses; the gutters are full of fœtid fluid; the clay-soil is covered, in many parts, by water, and the whole surface is muddy. Around the square are collections of garbage, and heaps of dust and ashes; the privies are full and offensive. It is stated that the dustman never comes to remove the refuse though repeatedly applied to. The houses are four-roomed, and are let to two families; for the ground-floor 3s. a week is the rent, for the floor above, 3s. 6d The water is supplied to this court from a sunk tank communicating with the main. A pump in the centre of the square raises the water when wanted.

NEW TYSSEN-ST., 58.—This street is in process of paving, but is as present in a most abominable state of dirt. No. — in this street has afforded an excelent illustration of the interest which is taken by the proprietors of small tenements to preserve their property from decay, and their tenants from disease. Not till the one has become dilapidated, and the other profitless, do they manifest that interest which it is their moral duty to display, and the neglect of which is entailing uepon a squalid population disease, premature decay, poverty, immorality, and irreligion. Five persons occupied this dwelling, and were successively attacked with fever; they were all removed to the workhouse. Two other persons again occupied the dwelling, and in turn succumbed to the insidious poison which haunted it; they likewise were removed to the fever wards of the workhouse. Again, a third family of two persons made their home in this place, and again the potent poison manifested its power, and prostrated the occupants with loathsome feve r—again did the workhouse receive the victims of disgraceful negligence and cruel apathy. Then, and not till then, was the foul and filthy cesspool emptied, and the drains, choked with solid filth, half cleansed; and when the work was done, and the foul smells still hung about the place, indicating the persistence of the poisonous agency, another family instantly, and in complete ignorance of the calamity impending over them, occupied the thrice-stricken abode.

GARDEN-PLACE, HOPE-TOWN, 59.—This place is in a lamentable condition; a narrow alley or lane separates the houses on either side; there is no drainage; therefore the place is damp and dirty. There are the usual collections of dust, ashes, and garbage; the privies are full, and many are most offensive. In one No. 8) the surface-drain (a wooden one) from the cesspool of No. 29, New Tyssen-street, which is immediately behind it, runs right below the wooden floor, which is rotten in some parts; 15 inches deep by 10 broad of half-dried fœcal matter were contained in it; the house itself was damp. The influence upon health of such a nuisance is illustrated in the remarks upon New Tyssen-street. It is utterly impossible that any population can be healthy in such a locality.

GOSSETT-ST., 60.—This street is so muddy, and so cut up, that the footpath is a quagmire, and the roadway impassable.

REFORM-SQ., MOUNT-ST., 61.—This is one of the cleanest courts in the district; besides a dust-heap in a corner, there are two privies, which are nearly full; there is one water-pipe without a cock to the six houses. As the court, however, is paved, the run of water from the open pipe, when it comes on, is very useful in cleansing the drain in the court.

LENHAM-BUILDINGS, MOUNT-ST., 62.—There is a dust-heap here; one pipe without a cock supplies seven houses.

MOUNT-SQ., 63.—The whole place is very dirty indeed; there are two privies in a beastly condition, and a refuse-heap in a recess in the back yard. The houses here are two-roomed, one above the other; the place is dark and dismal. One pipe without a cock supplies the place with water. A slaughter-house abuts on this square, the smell from which is complained of by the inhabitants as most dreadful and scarcely endurable; the blood of the slaughtered animals is stated to be retained in holes for a week or a fortnight together; the untrapped drain in the centre of the square likewise, occasionally, creates most offensive smells. At least a dozen cases of fever have been attended by the parochial medical officer in this court during the last twelve months, besides scarlet fever, &c. Nine years ago; a similar story was told by Dr. Smith. He then stated, on the authority of the then parochial medical officer, that seven persons were attacked in succession in No. 2, six in No. 3; in the next house three, and in the next one. For nine years, then, at least, has this court continued to do its work in poisoning by fever the unfortunate poor who ignorantly take up their abode in this nest of fever. How long shall it be permitted thus to injure the health and destroy the lives of its occupants?

TURVILLE-PL., 64.—There is one stand-pipe, with stop-cock, for the whole court.

ROOK'S-PL., GIBRALTAR-WALK, 65.—In this place is a very extensive contractor's yard; as about 100 horses are kept in this yard, very considerable accumulations of manure take place, which are not regularly removed; two enormous cart-loadsfull were being removed at the time of my visit. The place is dirty; five families reside in this yard; by its side is the nuisance referred to under the head of Turk-street, 39.

COTTAGE-PL., SATCHWELL-RENTS, 66.—Here there are one stand-tap to three houses, and a refuse-heap.

MOUNT-PL., 67.—Here there is a dust-heap; one stand-tap is outside, and three taps are in the cupboards of the houses, which render them damp; the privies are full.

DISTRICT, No. 4.

Streets, Courts, and Alleys, &c.	Number of Houses	Footpath F.	Footpath Paved P.	Granite Roadway G.	Street Drainage D.	Sewerage S.	Street Clean C.	Sts. dirty or very dirty d vd	Gutters full or ovrflwing gf	Privies full or overflowing pf	Nuisances, refer to figures	Dths from fvr in 12 mnths	Dths from othr zymotic dis.	Cass of fvr attd by med offic	Cs of zymotic dis in 12 ms.	Courts C, Alleys A, Cul-de-sacs Cul, Private P, Gardens G.
Albion-place, Duke-street		F	P					vd		pf	40		1	1		Alley.G
Austin-street	2	F	P		D			vd	gf		10					
Bakers-court, Virginia-row		F	P								14			1		C.
Boreham-street		F	P	G	D		C						2		1	
Boundary-st., in this parish		F	P	G	D			vd	gf		21		3	1	5	
Brenan's-pl., Gibraltar-walk								vd		pf	53					Alley.
Broadway, Austin-street		F	P		D	S		vd	gf		20					
Charlotte-ct., Turville-st		F	P	G				d								C.
Charlotte-st., Nichol's-row		F	P	G				d	gf					4	1	
Charlotte-st., Hope-town		F	P	G			C									Alley.
Church-st., N. W. of do. do.		F	P	G	D	S		vd	gf				2	2	1	
Collingwood-pl., Mount-st		F			D			d		pf	16				3	C.
Collingwood and Little do st		F			D			vd	gf		17		5	6	4	
Coopers-gdns & Carters-rts		F	P		D						9	1	1		3	Alley.
Crabtree-row		F	P					vd			7	1	3	6	2	
Cottage-place		F	P								66					C.
Crescent-place		F	P				C				5		1			Cul.
Cross-street, Hart's-lane		F	P					vd	gf							
Cross-street, Nelson-street		F			D			d	gf						5	
Cross-street, Old Nichol-st		F	P	G				vd	gf							
Daniel-street, Orange-street		F						d	gf						2	Cul.
Devonshire-pl, old Nichol-st	9	F	P	G				vd	gf		33			1	2	C. Cul.
Duke-street, Turk-street		F						vd	gf				2		2	
Eleanor-place, Newcastle-st																C.
Elizabeth-pl., Crabtree-road	5				D			d								Alley
Fountain-alley, do. do.	2							vd	gf							Alley.
Fountain-court, do. do.	2															Alley.
Friars Mount, or Mount-st		F	P					vd	gf				3	2	11	
Garden-place, Hope-town		F	P					d	gf	pf	59		1	2	3	
Gascoigne-place		F	P	G				vd	gf		8		1	1	6	
George-street, Hope-town		F	P	G	D		C									
Gibraltar-gardens		F	P		D		C	d	gf		56	1	1			G.
Gibraltar-place		F	P		D		C				55		1			
Gibraltar-walk		F	P		D			vd	gf		52	1	3	2	8	
Godfrey's-place, Austin-st		F	P		D				gf							Cul.
Gosset-st., King-street		F						vd	gf		60					
Green-gate-gardens								vd		pf	23		1	2	3	G Alley
Gt. Collingwood-street																
George-terrace, Turville-st		F	P		D		C				28		2			
Hackney-rd, N W of Chas-st		F	P		D	S	C								1	

DISTRICT, No. 4.

Streets, Courts, and Alleys, &c.	Number of Houses.	Footpath F.	Footpath Paved P.	Granite Roadway G.	Street Drainage D.	Sewerage S.	Streets Clean C.	Sts. dirty or very dirty d vd.	Gutters full or overflwng g. gf.	Privies full or overflowing pf.	Nuisances refer to figures.	Deaths from fever in 12 ms.	Dths frm other zymotic dis.	Cases of fvr attd by med offr.	Cs of othr zymtic dis in 12 ms	Courts C, Alleys A, Cul-de sacs Cul, Private P, Gardens G.
Half Nichol-street		F.	P.	G.				vd	gf.		29		2	8	12	
Hepworth-pl., Fountain-ally	15							vd		pf.	43				2	C.
King-st., Wt. of Hart's-lane		F.						vd	gf.					1		
King-street, Hackney-road		F.						vd	gf.	pf.						
King's place, do. do.	6	F.	P.					vd	gf.	pf.						
King-st., Turk-street		F.			D.			vd	gf.	pf.				3	2	
Lemon-ct., Old Nichol-st.	4	F.	P.	G.			C.									
Lenham-bldgs, Mount-st.	7	F.	P.				C.			pf.	62					
Little Gascoigne-place		F.	P.		D.			vd		pf.						
Maidstone-pl, Old Nichol-st	2							vd	gf.	pf.	32					
Mead-st., Vincent-street		F.	P.	G.				vd	gf.	pf.	25	1				
Miring-place, Nelson-street	8							vd		pf.	15		1			C.
Montague-st., Union-street								vd	gf.				1	1		
Mount-square		F.	P.					vd	gf.	pf.	63	1				
Mount-place							C.	vd		pf.	67				3	
Nelson and Little Nelson-st		F.	P.					vd	gf.	pf.	18	3	7	13		
Newcastle-street		F.	P.	G.			C.		gf.				1	1		
New-ct., New Nichol-street	5	F.	P.								35					C.
New Nichol-street		F.	P.	G.				vd	gf.		34		2	9	10	
New-st., Boundary-street		F.	P.	G.				vd	gf.							
New-street, Mount-street		F.	P.						gf.							
New-street, Turk-street		F.						vd	gf.				2	1	4	
New Turville-street		F	P.		D.			rd	gf.							
New Tyssen-street		F	P.		D.			vd	gf.	pf.	58			1	6	
Nichols-row		F	P.	G.					dgf.		24	1		2		
Norton-gdns, Gibraltar-wlk	6				D.			vd		pf.	51					Alley.
Old Castle-court		F.	P.		D.			vd	gf.	pf.	12				1	C.
Old Castle-street		F.	P.		D.	S.		vd	gf.		11	5		F	14	
Old Nichol-street		F.	P	G				vd	gf.			2		6	7	
Orange-ct., Old Nichol-st.	5	F.	P				C.									C.
Orange-street		F.						vd	gf.			1	2	1		
Peter-street, Rose-street		F.		G.				vd	gf.							
Pierces-place, Fountain-ally								vd		pf.	44					C.
Princes-court, Tyssen-street		F.			D.				dgf.					1	10	C.
Princes-court, Virginia-row	20				D.				dgf.	pf.	42		5	6		C.
Princes-place, Turk-street	4								dgf.	pf.			1	1		Alley.
Princes-street, Duke-street								vd	gf.					3	9	
Providence-place, do. do.	8	F.			D.		C.	d			41					Alley.
Queens-place		F.	P.		D.				dgf.			1				
Reform-square, Mount-st.	6	F.	P.		D.		C.				61					Alley.

DISTRICT, No. 4.

Streets, Courts, and Alleys, &c.	Number of Houses.	Footpath F.	Footpath Paved P	Granite Roadway G.	Street Drainage D.	Sewered S.	Streets Clean C.	Sts. dirty or very dty v d	Gutters full or ovrflwng gf.	Privies full or ovrflwng pf.	Nuisances refer to figures.	Dcths from fever in 12 ms.	Dths frm other zymotic dis	Cas of fevr attd by md offr	Css of zymotic dis in 12 ms	Corts C, Allys A, Cul-de-sacs Cul, Private P, Gardens G.
Rose-place, Turk-street	5		P.					vd	gf.	pf.	39					C.
Rose-street		F.	P.	G.				d	gf.		37		6	4	2	
Rooks-place	6	F.	P.		D.			d	gf.		65					
Sarah-street, Vincent-street		F.	P.					d	gf.							
Satchwell-rents, Church-st.		F.	P.		D.			vd	gf.						1	
Satchwell-st., do. do.		F.	P.	G.	D.			d	gf.						4	
Seven-step, or Crown-court	4							vd		pf.	46				1	C.
Shacklewell-st, Tyssen-st.		F.	P.	G.	D.			vd	gf.	pf.	36		3	7	8	Cul.
Shepherd's-ct Old Nichol-st	6	F.						vd	gf.	pf.	31			11		
Sherwood-place, Nelson-st.		F.	P.	G.	D.			d	gf.					2	2	Cul.
Short-st., New Nichol-st.		F.	P.	G.				vd	gf.		23				1	
Smith's-bldgs., *		F.	P.					d	gf.		51		1	7	1	
Smith's-place, King-street		F.						vd	gf.	pf.	50				7	P.
Somerset-bldgs, Clarence-pl								d	gf.	pf.	6		2		1	Garden
Strout-place †		F.			D.			vd	gf.	pf.	49					
Sweet Apple-court			P.					d	gf.	pf.	13				2	C.
Thomas-pl., Old Nichol-st	4	F.	P.	G.			C.				30					Cul.
Thorold-square	22				D.			vd	gf.	pf.	57		1	1	6	
Trafalgar-st., Nichols-row		F.		G.				vd	gf.		9					
Turk-court		F.	P.	G.				d	gf.							
Turk-street		F.	P.	G.				d	gf.		38		7	5	8	
Turville-buildings					D.					pf.	27				2	C.
Turville-place		F.	P.		D.			d		pf.	64		2			C.
Turville-street		F.	P.	G.				vd	gf.		26		2		5	
Tyrrell-street, Hope-town		F.	P.		D.		C.						1	1		
Tyssen-street		F.	P.	G.				d	gf.				4	1	1	
Thomas-place Crabtree-row								vd		pf.	45					C.
Union-street, Hope-town		F.	P.		D.		C.								1	
Victoria-st., Coopers-gards		F.	P.					vd				4	1			
Virginia-row		F.	P.	G.	D.	S.		vd	gf.				6	5	12	
Vincent-street		F.	P.	G.				vd	gf.				3	4	12	
Weatherhead-gardens	22							vd	gf.		47					G.
Wells-court, Clarence-place		F.	P.				C.				48					C.
Willow-walk		F.	P.		D.			d	gf.		1		2		2	

* Called also Stepney Rents, Powell-place, or Baker's Rents
† See also 4.

DISTRICT, No. 5.

This district is by far the most respectable of the five medical parochial districts. It contains the main road and the streets branching from it. The unhealthiest parts are Cambridge Circus, Chapman's-gardens, Bath-street, and part of Old Bethnal Green-road; there are no nuisances in it except the remarkable one referred to under the head of Anne's-place; the drainage in the best part is pretty good, though still capable of great improvement,—there are comparatively few weavers occupying this district. These two elements tend to reduce the mortality and amount of disease; the remarkable exemption of the chief parts of this district from fever and the other epidemic diseases, is no doubt to be attributed to the comparative cleanliness and good drainage; this last is chiefly to be attributed to the natural levels of the district. Great complaints however arise in consequence of part of the main road being unprovided with a sewer. Some of the best houses in the district are thus compelled to have privies and cesspools greatly against the inclination of the occupants. Several of the parties residing in this unsewered part of the road, were Commissioners of Sewers, but could never induce that obstructive, overbearing body to attend to their wants. The new houses built in Peter-street and Elizabeth-place, are very well drained and are supplied with water-closets. A thing so extremely rare as to be worthy of observation, probably there are more water closets attached to these few houses, than there are in all the other thousands of houses in the parish.

ANN'S-PLACE, 1.—Leading from it to the space near the canal, is an open field, where there are several open foul drains and ditches.

Since the delivery of my Lecture, the following nuisance has become established this place. Between the canal and the back of St. Matthew's-place, Hackney-road, entering from Anne's-place, a nightman has formed reservoirs for every conceivable kind of filth. One covers a triangular space of ground, the sides of which respectively measure 177, 126, and 114 feet; the dung, refuse, filth, &c., are piled up to a considerable height, except where the contents of the cesspools are thrown. By the side of this triangle, leading from Anne's-place, there is a ditch, filled with most offensive and putrid matters, precisely the same as in Lamb's-fields; it is about 390 feet long, and varies from three to sixteen feet in width. At a right angle there branches from it a smaller, but equally filthy ditch, about 300 yards long. Where these filthy ditches meet they form a broad moat round a hillock of refuse, the matter of which, sliding into the moat, affords a constant supply of material to keep up offensive and destructive decomposition. In taking notice of this frightful and pestilential nuisance, I have not taken into consideration two or three mountainous heaps of ashes, cinders, &c., which are not positively offensive and noxious; the odour given off from this place is beyond conception disgusting—it spreads to a great distance, and is complained of by all as an intolerable nuisance. *

* ANN's PLACE, 1.—While passing this sheet through the press, I again visited the nuisance in Ann's-place, and found that considerable changes had very recently been effected. Such nuisances are, in truth, generally in a transition state. The manure has been shipped in barges, a great part of the ditches has been filled up, and the refuse sorted into matter for burning, and for making bricks. A filthy open privy with the excreta draining into a ditch, presents a very repulsive aspect. The manure is now, I was told by a workman, chiefly sent to a depôt of his master's in Worship-street. The neighbourhood complains greatly of the constant transit of wagons of filth.

No one, I believe, whatever may be their opinion as to the nuisance in St. Luke's which lately came under judicial interference, could possibly doubt that such enormous heaps of decaying animal and vegetable remains must prove injurious to health. The senses revolt, the feelings are roused with indignation and depressed by despair, when such atrocities are seen perpetrated in the very face of society. The laws which imprison and transport for petty theft, view with calm indifference this wholesale, barefaced, and violent robbery of the health of communities. People, helpless and impotent, cry out in puerile indignation against such abominable and pestilential conservations of refuse; but, the sordid gainers, firm and entrenched in the strongholds of legal quirks, and laxity, and the astounding indifference of governmental and local authorities, set their feeble cries of suffering and despair at defiance.

The existence of these nuisances in Bethnal Green, so long after the passing of Lord Morpeth's Act for "the removal of nuisances," clearly indicates that the task of their suppression must be laid upon some public functionary.

CHAPMAN'S-GARDEN'S, CAROLINE-PLACE, AND QUEEN CAROLINE-PLACE, 2—A the foot of Seabright-street, and in these gardens, there is a stable and pigstye, which usually emits a most offensive smell; the dung is stored and laid on the surface of the neighbouring damp, and totally undrained, plots of ground; sometimes it is dug into the ground. There are 20 houses comprised in these gardens, three of which have water laid on, the remaining 17 require to obtain it from a common stand-pipe, the cock of which has been cut off. When the water comes on, therefore, it is allowed to run till turned off from the main; the narrow footpath is thereby flooded, and the road made miry. In wet weather the whole of this place is very dirty; the houses are necessarily very damp. Queen Caroline-place, and Caroline-place, are the southern part of these gardens, and entered by a distinct lane, the houses here (with the exception of two which are good, in the best the owner of the other houses live,) are of the same description as those in Gale's and George-gardens. Most of the houses have a separate supply of water; some, however, have only one pipe common to two; barrels sunk into the ground receive the water in some instances. The privies are full, and drain into a cesspool close by them. In the house I entered the cesspool was kept uncovered, in order to allow the smell to escape, in the belief that the drainage was promoted by the access of air; the drainage of these houses consists of a four inch brick drain, generally dilapidated and broken down,—and frequently stopped up; the place is complained of, as being grievously damp.

PAIN'S-GARDENS, 3.—A court containing seven houses inhabited by weavers. One house has no water supply, the occupants therefore, beg or steal it; there are three taps to the other six houses, the privies are dilapidated, full, and most offensive. There is no drainage whatever, its want is greatly complained of; £12 a year are paid for each of these dirty houses which has a work-room above and two small rooms below. Disease is exceedingly rife in this filthy place.

TEALE-ST., 4.—Behind this row of houses and in process of being filled up, is a very deep and very extensive hollow, the result of an excavation for clay, to make bricks, made more than twenty years ago. Into this hole all the small drains of the neighbourhood lead; every kind of refuse is thrown into it, eight privies empty their contents into it, and dead animals putrefy there; the smell from this place is most offensive and disgusting; next to Lamb's-fields this nuisance is (or rather was) one of the most vile. A shallow surface drain conveys the excess of the contents of this hole through No. 10, Goldsmith-row, into a sewer made two years ago, in Goldsmith-row; the houses in this row are distant only eight feet from it: the yards being bounded by it. Previously to the formation of the sewer in Goldsmiths-row, and now, when the surface drain is stopped up, the stagnant fœtid putrid fluid floods the houses to a depth of ten or twelve inches. When I examined No. 10, I found the marks of the levels of the former inundations. Water is supplied to these houses and retained in open barrels, it is therefore exposed to the foul air and poisonous miasma, arising from this putrescent pond. The house itself consists of three rooms,—the kitchen is under the level of the road, six feet high, and seven feet wide, and eight long; the surface drain passes just under the surface. The work-room is seven and-a-half feet high, and eight feet wide, the bed-room above is the same size, but has a sloping roof—in this room a man, his wife and mother sleep.

The occupants complain of constant nausea, and loss of appetite, headache, and general debility, and indisposition; their sallow unhealthy countenances sufficiently indicate the pernicious effects upon their health, of the poison which they are constantly inhaling. It is proper to add, that this nuisance is not in the parish of Bethnal-green, but only just without it. The deleterious emanations which arise from it, however, affecting as they do the health of the neighbourhood, necessitate an account of it.

In front of Teale-street is a large open space used by the public to deposit garbage, refuse, dirt, and filth of all descriptions, which are seldom, if ever, removed. This place constitutes an offensive nuisance.

Emma-st., 5.—Opposite to this new street, and behind St. Matthew's-place, Hackney-road, is an immense lake, the result of the filling up by springs and drainage of an enormous excavation, made twenty or thirty years ago to procure clay for bricks; this lake has been infinitely more offensive than at the present time, but even now constitutes a great nuisance. Much refuse drains and is thrown into it. It should be made compulsory on the owners of such property to fill up the excavations, which they make, in order to prevent them becoming putrid lakes and intolerable nuisances.

Oval, 6.—Near the entrance to these cottages, there is a dairy, with the customary accumulation of dung and refuse; the houses here are damp, especially those on the western side, bordering the lake just spoken of.

Grove-row, 7.—Is a long, very narrow alley, bounded by high walls on both sides, leading from the Oval to the Canal. In Grove-row, there are five houses on the right side of a tolerably fair character,—but further on to the left, there are four miserable one-storied, two-roomed houses; there are no back yards to these houses, which enter upon the alley, but at the end (likewise opening into the alley, but separate from the houses), there is one small yard in which are contained two large butts, which afford an excellent supply of water; there is one privy and one dust heap here for the four houses; this alley is a perfect nuisance, it serves as a common convenience, it is always muddy and dirty, and covered with garbage and excrements.

Hare-row, 8.—Consists of eleven houses, three of which face Cambridge-place, the roadway before these is always in the most disgraceful condition, covered with garbage, and very offensive; the scavengers never cleanse this place, at least it has not been cleansed, according to the occupants, for the last three years. Eight houses lay back from Grove-row and have plots of ground in front of them; these plots or yards are muddy and dirty; three houses have a separate supply of water and privy, the next three houses have one stand-pipe in common, the next two have each a supply of water. To these five houses there are three privies in a very fair condition as to external cleanliness, but still offensive; there is one dust-bin common to the five houses.

Center-street, 9.—Along one side of the street, and close to the footpath, are the other privies of the houses in front of it.

Albion-buildings, 10.—These are tolerably fair houses, the back yards to these houses are damp, dust-heaps and garbage-heaps are common, and the whole place looks dilapidated; there is a privy to each house, and a large cesspool common to two privies,—that which I visited was nearly full and offensive but was considered by the occupants in a perfectly satisfactory state, and quite uno jectionable. I am firmly convinced that, to the filthy state of the yards is to be attributed the amount of sickness in this place.

Accidental-place, 11.—Consists of three small houses, each two-roomed, and one story; the rooms are ten feet long by eight broad, and about seven and a-half or eight feet high. There is one very small yard in common to the first two houses; there is also one stand-pipe in common, there is a privy to each house, full, and filthy; also a small wash-house six feet by four feet, in the most dilapidated condition possible; there is a large dust and garbage heap in the yard. When the water comes on, unless some person is at home to attend to it, the water comes into the house; the last house has no supply of water, but is empty at present. In the first of these wretched habitations, a mother and her six children reside; the husband is from home, but a person keeps house with her. Eight persons, therefore, sleep in the bed-room. The children look ill and sickly. In No. 2, a man, his wife, and child reside; the two former are recovering from fever. The small passage in front of these houses is six feet wide, it is covered with garbage, and in wet weather is abominably filthy, as usual it is never cleansed. A dead wall is in front, and at the end, of this cul-de-sac; three shillings a week is the rent of each of these hovels.

Nelson-place, 12.—A narrow blind alley, which has six houses at the upper end, and ten at the lower; these ten have small yards in front of them, they are two-roomed, and one story high,—the rooms are about ten feet broad by nine deep, and seven feet and a-half or eight feet high; there is a small back-yard to each house, about four feet by five, less the space occupied by a privy; the privies drain away, probably into cesspools, as there is no sewer here,—there is a dirty heap in each yard. The privies are dirty and so are the yards. Each house has a tap; the houses at the end of this alley are very damp; the alley itself is dirty and covered in various parts with dust-heaps and garbage; there is a dead wall in front of the houses, and at the end of the alley; the privies of the neighbouring houses abut on the wall. At the end of it, the contents of the privies attached to the houses in the Hackney-road, had oozed through the wall, and covered the alley. A quantity of dirt and refuse was thrown upon it, to conceal its offensiveness; the place has been in this state for at least three months. The inhabitants complained grievously of the offensive smells emitted by the privies in front of their houses. The following table exhibits the state of this alley:—

No.	No. of Inhab.	—	—	Exposed to foul smells from the privies in front of them.
16	8	The soakage from the privy in Hackney-road covers this part of the alley.		No.16: 2 rheumatic
15	4			No.15, 1 had cholera
14	9		The privies drain below the floors, soak them, and render the walls and floors very damp; so much so, that if the floors are washed, they can with great difficulty be dried, even with the aid of a good fire.	No. 13,—4 persons complained of nausea and loss of appetite.
13	3			
12	4	The soakage from the privy behind the house fills the fire-place of the small wash-house, and is covered over with cinders to *conceal* it.		
11	4			
10	4			No. 9—2 children lately died, one of congestion of brain.
9	5			
8	1			
7	0			No 7—Wife in hospital.
6	6			
5	4			
4	7			
3	4			
2	6			
1	0			

AMY'S-PLACE, 13.—A narrow passage with three houses on either side, the alley is damp and dirty, the houses are two-roomed and one story high; they have a back-yard eight feet by four feet, a collection of dirt and garbage, and a privy nearly full. The houses are very damp, and the inhabitants say that the place strikes cold like a well; those which I saw were all suffering from severe catarrh. Three shillings a week is the rent of these houses, little better than those in Accidental-place.

PROVIDENCE-PLACE, 14.—An alley leading from Bath-street to Barnet-street; the drain passes under the floor of No. 6, and renders it very damp.

BATH-ST., 15.—This street is very dirty, and the surface broken up and covered with all kinds of refuse and garbage.

JAMES-ST., 16.—Two of the houses in this street were originally summer-houses, in gardens.

CROSS-ST., BARNET-ST., 17.—The houses here are damp, a small part of the footpath is paved,—garbage abounds on the street.

BARNET-GROVE, 18.—This street is always remarkably dirty; the houses are damp, many of them being planted in small *gardens*.

WILLOW-WALK, BARNET-GROVE, 19.—This is a long narrow alley, about 200 yards long, leading to the Baker's Arms public house, in Warner-place; there are five houses on the northern side of it, and about sixteen on the southern side; three of the former and eight of the latter are in small gardens. For 77 yards in this *most filthy walk*, does a stagnant fœtid gutter extend. In wet weather the contents are washed over the road, and render it almost impassable. I recollect seeing here some cases of very malignant scarlatina. The houses in the gardens have water laid on, and the privies drain into cesspools in the centre of the gardens. Between Willow-walk and the back of the houses in part of Barnet-street, and behind Ion-square, are two rope walks, north of these rope walks, and commencing close to where Barnet-grove joins Barnet-street, is a black ditch, or open sewer, filled with most offensive putrid refuse and mud, it runs westwards 170 yards in a straight line, and is from four to five and six feet wide, at the western end it receives the contents of five or six privies, and at the eastern end it spreads itself out and cover about 30 feet square, with its putrescent slime.

BOURN'S OR BAKER'S ARMS GARDENS, 20.—These gardens occupy a large space between Warner-place and Barnet-grove; they are in an intermediate state between George and Gale's-gardens on the one hand, and Whisker's-gardens on the other. By far the greater number of summer-houses, or wooden sheds in these gardens are unoccupied, still a considerable number are inhabited; the majority of those which are inhabited are, however, of a better character and seem to have been somewhat adapted for the residence of human beings. Water is laid on to the houses on the outskirts, but there is no drainage whatever, except into cesspools; the necessaries are either common privies, or privies draining into cesspools, the whole place is excessively damp. In summer these gardens present an appearance remarkable for their beautiful flowers and their general neatness.

WELLINGTON-ROW, 21.—A street entirely occupied by weavers, the street itself is very dirty and the gutters full; the houses are of the usual construction of weavers houses, and of course greatly defective as regards ventilation. The north side of this street consists of cottages and gardens, which are generally neatly laid out.

WELLINGTON-PLACE, 22.—There is no proper footpath here, the gutter is generally full from the drain at the end being stopped up, and the whole of the public way exceedingly filthy and dirty from that cause, and from being on a lower level than the adjoining street, called James-street; this place is chiefly occupied by weavers; there is an open space in front of the houses where the public deposit all kinds of refuse and garbage, and create an offensive nuisance.

HAMMOND-GARDENS, 23.—A court containing seven houses, with small yards in front, one large dust and garbage heap occupies a principal part of the entrance way, there is but one privy to all the houses, and one butt to supply them with water.

CLAREMONT COTTAGES AND LANSDOWNE-PLACE, 24.—Are each a row of nine houses in a court, which appears clean, being unpaved, however, the ground readily becomes muddy and dirty.

SIMPSON-PLACE, WEST AND EAST, 25.—Are entered by distinct alleys. Simpson-place, West, contains four two-roomed, one storied houses, each with a small yard, wash-house, privy and water supply, and the usual dust heap. It likewise contains eleven houses, two-roomed, and one-storied, with no back yards whatever; the yards or gardens are in front of the houses and are under water whenever rain falls, dust heaps and garbage abound in this yard. One stand pipe supplies the eleven houses; there is no cock to it; there is one privy at each end of the alley in a better condition than such places usually are; three shillings and sixpence are the rent of each of the former four comparatively comfortable houses. Simpson's-place, East, contains twenty-three houses. Six are similar to the four in Simpson's-place, West, but are let at 4s. 8d. a week; two are similar to the eleven referred to, have one privy, in common, and one stand pipe; they have two heaps of dust and refuse, and garbage; the other fifteen houses are intermediate in their state between these two kinds of houses; the very small back yards contain a privy, and the inhabitants complain grievously of the offensiveness arising from its proximity. Many of the yards in front are *under water*, all are *very damp*.

ION-SQUARE, 26.—Thirty-eight new houses, forming three sides of a square. Close by the southern end runs the filthy black ditch spoken of under the head of Willow-walk. Nearly all the houses in this square are remarkably damp, so much so as to be very injurious to health.

HILL-ST., 27.—A cross-street, behind a part of Hackney-road, and considerably below its level; thirteen of the houses are below the level of the street, and require to have a raised gutter to prevent the contents flowing into them.

WOLVERLEY-ST., 28.—A double row of houses forming a cul-de-sac; they are placed on a low level, and are very damp. Ventilation is imperfect here.

BADEN-PLACE, 29.—These houses are situated on the northern bank of the canal on a very low level; the whole of these houses and the houses behind them, in the parish of Hackney are exceedingly damp; the streets are in the worst condition possible, from the total want of drainage, and abounding with impurities and stagnant water. Fever, rheumatism, catarrh, and zymotic diseases are especially common.

SHEEP-LANE, 30.—An unmade roadway, and probably the worst in London.

SOUTHAMPTON-COTTAGES, 31.—Six small houses at the back of Southampton-place, unusually well provided with domestic accommodations, but being much below the level of the surrounding neighbourhood they are very damp.

CAROLINE-ST., HACKNEY-ROAD, 32.—A long narrow street, dark and ill-ventilated.

DISTRICT, No. 5.

Streets, Courts, and Alleys, &c.	Number of Houses.	Footpath F.	Footpath Paved P.	Granite Roadway G.	Street Drainage D.	Sewered S.	Streets Clean C.	Sts. dirty or very dirty v vd.	Gutters full or overflowing gf	Privies full or overflowing pf	Nuisances, refer to figures.	Dths from fever in 12 mths.	Dths from other zymotic dis.	Cas of fever attd by med off	Cases of zymotic dis in 12 ms	Courts C., Alleys A, Cul-de-sacs Cul, Private P, Gardens G.
Abbey-pl., Old Beth-gr-rd.		F.							d gf.							
Accidental-place, Bath-st.	3			D.				vd	gf.	pf.	11					A, Cul.
Ada-street, Ann's-place	7								d							Cul.
Albion-buildings	15	F.							d	gf.	pf.	10		1	2	4
Amy's-place, Bath-street	6								vd	gf.	pf.	13				A, Cul.
Ann's-place	60	F.				S.			vd	gf.		1	1	1	1	1
Baden-place, Canal-side		F.							d	gf.		29		1		
Barnet-street		F.	P.				C.						1	3	2	
Bath-street		F.	P.		D.				vd	gf.		15				
Barnet-grove		F.							vd	gf.		18			2	
Bakers Arms or Bourn's-gar							C.				pf.	20				G.
Cambridge-circus		F.		D.					d	gf.				1		1
Cambridge-place		F.		D.			C.		d	gf.						
Catherine-street	22	F.													1	
Chapman's-gardens	33								d	gf.	pf.	2		1	1	1	G.
Center-street	26	F.							d	gf.		9		1		2
Chapel-street		F.							d	gf.				1		
Charles-street, Hackney-rd.		F.					C.									
Charles-street, Temple-st.		F.					C.							1		Cul.
Claremont Cottages	9	F.					C.					24				Cul.
Claremont-street							C.									
Clare-street	22	F.							d	gf.				1		2
Colcharbour-street		F.	P.						d	gf.				1		
Crescent Cottages, Canal							C.									
Caroline-street, Hackney-rd	36	F.	P.						d	gf.		32		1			A.
Cross-street, Barnet-street	14								vd	gf.		17	1			
Durham-street		F.					C.						1	1		
Elizabeth-street		F.							d	gf.						
Emma-street, Ann's-place	33								d	gf.		5	1	1		
Felix-street	14	F.							d	gf.			1	1	4	2
Gloucester-pl., Hackney-rd.		F.					C.			gf.						
Gloucester-street do		F.	P.				C.							1	1	
Grove-row, back of the Hare									d	gf.	pf.	7		1		
Hackney-rd, S.E.of Chas-st		F.	P.		D.S.									2		
Hammond's-gardens	7						C.					23				C.
Hare-row		F.	P.		D.				vd	gf.	pf.	8				2
Hope-street		F.	P.				C.			gf.					3	
Henrietta-street	32	F.					C.							1		2
Hill-street, Seabright-street	27								d	gf.		27				
Ion-square	38						C.					20				C.

DISTRICT No. 5.

Streets, Courts, and Alleys, &c.	Number of Houses.	Footpath F.	Footpath Paved P.	Granite Roadway G.	Street Drainage D.	Sewered S.	Streets Clean C.	Sts dirty or very dirty v vd.	Gutters full or overflowing gf Privies full or overflowing pf.	Nuisances, refer to figures.	Deaths from fever in 12 ms.	Dths frm other zymotic dis.	Cas of fvr att'd by med offrs.	Cas of zymotic dis. in 12 ms.	Courts C, Alleys A, Cul-de-sacs Cul, Private P, Gardens G.
James-street, Ravencroft-st.									d gf.	16					
Lansdowne-pl., Durham-st	9	F					C.			24					Cul.
London-street		F.	P.						d						
Minerva-street	64	F.					C.		d		1	4	3	7	
Matilda-street	28	F.							d gf.			1			
Nelson-place, Bath-street	16	F.						vd	gf. pf.	12				2	Alley.
Nelson-street, Hackney-rd.	32	F.	P.						d		2		1	3	
Old Bethnal-green-road					D.	S.					1	1			
Oval Cottages		F.					C.		d	6					
Peter-street, Hackney-road		F.	P.		D.	S.	C.					2	4		
Providence-place, Bath-st.					D.				d	14					
Pain's-gardens	7							vd	pf.	3		1	2	7	C.
Ravencroft-street		F.	P.						d						
Sebright-street									d gf.		2	2			
Sheep-lane, Canal, in parish								vd	gf.	30					Alley.
Sheldon-place, Elizabeth-st.							C.								Alley.
Simpson's-place, London-st	38								d gf. pf.	25		1			Alley.
Southampton Cotgs., Hy-rd.	6				D.		C.			31					Alley.
Spencer-passage	0								d gf.						Alley.
Teale-street					D.			vd	gf.	4				3	
Temple-street		F.							d gf.		1	1		1	
Warner-place		F.	P.		D.	S.	C.					1			
Wellington-place					D.				d gf.	22				1	
Wellington-row	22	F.			D.	S.		vd	gf.	21		2	1	2	
Willow-walk, Barnet-grove								vd	gf.	19					
Wolverley-street	39	F.							d gf.	28			1	2	C

SUMMARY

OF THE PRECEDING SKETCHES AND ILLUSTRATIONS

OF THE PARISH OF BETHNAL GREEN.

LOCATION AND STRUCTURE OF DWELLING-HOUSES.

SPACE ALLOTTED TO DWELLING-HOUSES.

HOUSE ACCOMMODATION.

LODGING HOUSES.

WARMING AND VENTILATION OF HOUSES.

VENTILATION OF PUBLIC BUILDINGS.

HOUSE CLEANSING.

——— BY DRAINAGE.

——— BY REMOVAL OF REFUSE.

PRIVIES AND CESSPOOLS.

PAVING.

STREET CLEANSING.

SEWERAGE.

INTERMENTS.

NUISANCES.

WATER SUPPLY.

SICKNESS AND DISEASE, AND MORTALITY.

TABLES ILLUSTRATING SICKNESS AND MORTALITY.

LOCATION AND STRUCTURE OF DWELLING-HOUSES.

" If these places are left to the casual or capricious amelioration of the humane even, ages will pass away, and, with them, a rapid succession of miserable generations, the most destitute of their species, perishing from corroding want, ere the decay of the buildings gives room for arrangements suitable to the accommodation of human beings."—Martin.—Report of the Health of Towns' Com.

These words applied to the towns of Nottingham, Coventry, Leicester, Derby, Norwich and Portsmouth, are unhappily not applicable to them alone, but apply with a truth the most profound, and a force the most powerful to the dwellings in many parts of Bethnal-Green.

It is lamentable to observe, in this extensive and populous parish, the enormous number of dwellings which have been constructed in defiance of every law and principle on which the health and lives of the occupants depend. In a vast number of instances, the dwellings have been planted, or stuck on the ground, with scarcely any foundation; great numbers have the clay, or damp ground, immediately below the wooden floors; they are very often below the level of the front or back-yards, or streets—from the first cause the rooms are excessively damp, and, in an extraordinary number of instances, truly uninhabitable; from the second cause, they are liable to be flooded, either on the occurrence of showers of rain, or when the water-pipes are left running. The dwellings are, in innumerable instances, considerably below the level of the whole of the surrounding neighbourhood, and are thus rendered very damp, as well as dark. House-drainage is almost an impossible thing under these circumstances;—for instance, all the houses behind Crabtree-row, and the filthy courts and dens abutting on it,—and those miserable remains of cabins and huts between Hackney Road, and the open space fronting Crabtree-row. The dwellings are often built of the worst materials, and thus become very speedily out of repair, a state in which they are allowed to remain as long as a tenant can be found for them. The roofs of the rooms I found, in a great number of instances, stained by the water which had percorated through the roofs of the houses; the inhabitants being thus exposed to the injurious effects of damp as well from above, as below. A very large proportion of the houses in this parish consist of two rooms, generally on the ground-floor; but in some instances they are placed one above the other. The door opens into one of these rooms, which is generally used by the occupants as a day-room and kitchen; the other is generally used as a sleeping-room for the whole family; the bed always takes up a great part of this room, and unfits it for habitual use.

The houses of the weavers generally consist of two rooms on the ground-floor and a workroom above; this workroom always has a large window for the admission of light during their long hours of sedentary labour. Whole streets of such houses abound in Bethnal-green, and a great part of the population is made up of weavers. There are some, but not a great number of, dwellings consisting of one room alone. Such dwellings are always of the worst description. Some parts of the parish, as districts, Nos. 3 and 4, abound in houses constructed in the French fashion,—flat upon flat. There is not any very great number of houses placed back to back; but those that are so placed are of an inferior kind, and are characterised by dirt and disease. For an example refer to Alfred-row, and Beckford-row, Devonshire-street, than which a more disgraceful, and unhealthy state of things can scarcely exist.

From the natural character of the soil in many parts of Bethnal-green, consisting of a stiff clay superimposed on a bed of gravel, or of a light, loose, porous surface, with water reached at the depth of a few feet, it would have appeared especially requisite that some efficient means should have been taken in the construction of houses to prevent the natural decay of the wooden floors often placed on, or within an inch or two of, the wet clay, and absorption by the walls of the wet. But the great majority of the houses occupied by the poorer classes in the Green and Church districts, and partly, also, in the Hackney-road district are so carelessly constructed and so indifferently maintained that they become prolific sources of disease. These kinds of houses afford the chief part of the occupation of the parochial medical officers.

The places which chiefly require animadversion, although the observations equally apply to numerous rows of houses called streets, are, in District No. 1, Whisker's-gardens, Martha-court, Helen's-place, James-place, and the courts and places attached to the various streets; in District No. 2, Gale's-gardens, Holly-bush-gardens, Camden-gardens, Smart's-gardens, Pleasant-row and place, Beckford-row, Thomas-row, Manchester-passage, Wilmot-grove, George-gardens, George-row, Falcon-court, Punderson's-gardens; in District No. 3, Granby-row, Swan-court, Busby-square and Busby-court; in District No. 4, Willow-walk, Greengate-gardens, Miring's-place, Hepworth-place, Smith's-place, Garden-place, Seven-step-court, Weatherhead-gardens, and many of the other courts and alleys; in District No. 5, several of the houses in Ann's-place, those in Chapman's-gardens, Pain's-gardens, Accidental-place, Nelson-place, Amy's-place, several of the houses in Barnet-street, most of those in Barnet-grove and Cross-street, all those in Willow-walk, and in Bourn's-gardens, and the observations are applicable in a great measure to Baden-place, and Ion-square.

SPACE ALLOTTED TO DWELLING-HOUSES.

Except in districts Nos. 3 and 4, where large houses and flats are common, and where space is comparatively valuable, back or front yards are attached to the great majority of the houses. It is very uncommon for the dwellings to be provided with both front and back yards; where the one is, the other is generally wanting. The immense majority of the back yards are extremely small, and are often greatly encroached upon by a privy. In the better class of houses a kind of washhouse is added to the dwelling, which still further encroaches upon the scanty space, usually allotted as a back yard. This space is generally the breadth of the house, by three or four feet deep. The front yards are common to a class of dwellings which are exceedingly general in Bethnal-green; namely, those which are termed gardens. These front yards usually occupy a space equal to that on which the house is built, and, in some gardens, are sufficiently large and convenient. They are, however, nearly, if not quite, peculiar to those kinds of dwellings. No inconsiderable number of the smaller houses in the parish have no back or front yards whatever, and are totally destitute of even the commonest conveniences; they are generally either in narrow streets or alleys, or else in courts.

HOUSE ACCOMMODATION.

The dwellings of the poor, in this parish, are, with very few exceptions, destitute of most of those structural conveniences common to the better classes of houses. There are never any places set aside for receiving coals; dust-bins to receive the refuse of the houses are exceedingly rare, and cupboards or closets are nearly altogether unknown. The privies (where there are any attached) are either close to the houses, or at a distance from it, exposed to the public view, or common to large numbers of houses and families. There are never any sinks. The fire-places are constructed without the slightest regard to the convenience or comfort of the inmates, and are altogether unadapted to successfully fulfil the purposes for which they were intended.

LODGING HOUSES.

I am not aware of any lodging-houses being situate in Bethnal-green. Nearly all the small public-houses and beer-shops, however, take in lodgers; and thus, on a small scale exhibit the evils common to lodging-houses.

That places of protection should be found for the vagrant population, and for that portion of the inhabitants of large towns, who, plunged in poverty, have no fixed home, is proved to be an essential duty of a well-constituted Government. This duty is essential, not less to protect the unfortunate, or abandoned, than to preserve the rest of the population from the physical disease and the frightful moral vices of which, in their present neglected condition, such dens of filth and moral degradation are foci. And, although in Bethnal-green such evils do not exist on the grand and comprehensive scale, nevertheless, each petty beer-shop, and public-house, especially in the Town, and part of the Hackney-road divisions, constantly exhibit the slow nurture, growth, and development of the same evils. The parochial medical officers complained to me, especially in No. 4 District, of the perpetual disease existing in these retreats of poverty and vice. Retrea s and dens which, in any measure which duly regards the public health, must be placed under public supervision. The keepers of such places must be required under a penalty, to give information to some duly constituted authority of every case of illness which confines an inmate to bed for

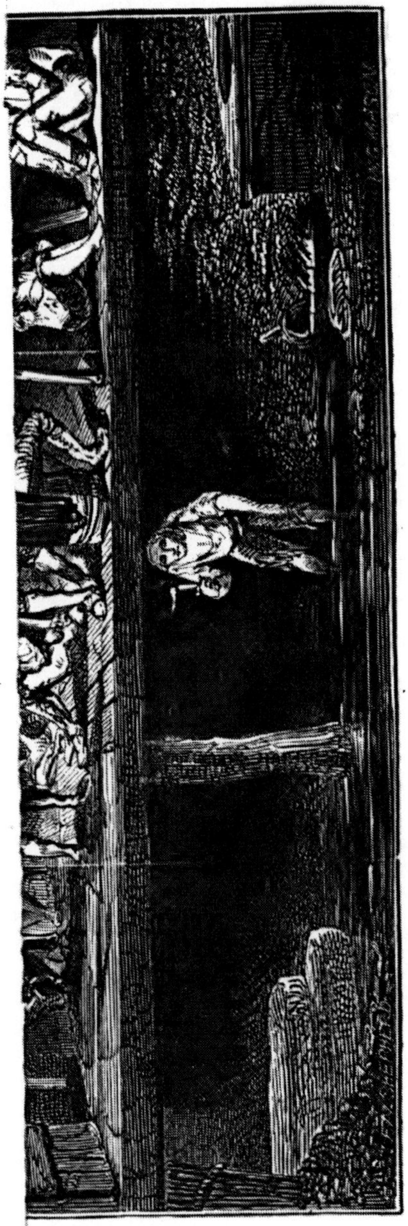

twenty-four hours, so that fever and the diseases which arise in them may be prevented from becoming sources of destruction to the neighbourhood, and of wasteful expense to the public. A power must likewise be given to shut up such places when their condition is such as to be injurious and dangerous to the public health.

Without such powers mere registration, or inspection, will be useless in checking disease.

By the kindness of the proprietor of the "POOR MAN'S GUARDIAN," I am enabled to insert the accompanying Wood-cut of a Lodging-house in Field-lane, which originally appeared in that periodical. It exemplifies the miserable conditions of such dens, which, in one form or another, are common to all crowded and poor localities.

WARMING AND VENTILATION.

Warming is necessarily connected with ventilation; no arrangements can be made for the one which do not necessarily complicate the other. In the construction of the dwellings of the poor, regard must be had as to some means of getting rid of the products of combustion, and of the air vitiated by respiration and by other causes, more efficient than the present imperfect fire-flue alone; and some efforts are imperatively demanded to *adapt* the *present* chambers of the poor, so that more perfect ventilation may take place. Whether these efforts shall partake of governmental interference, or shall be confined to example and precept; those, only, who are fully aware of the difficulties inherent to the subject can determine. But that to maintain and preserve the health of the great mass of the poor, who dwell and work in doors, more efficient means of ventilation are absolutely required, it would be a waste of time, to attempt to prove. Probably ventilation is not in a worse state in Bethnal-green than in all other similar districts, but as the parish contains a proportionately greater number of persons who derive their livelihood by in door occupations, the subject of ventilation becomes of more importance to them than to their neighbours.

The air which is breathed within the dwellings of the poor is often most insufferably offensive to strangers. It is loaded with the most unhealthy emanations from the lungs and persons of the occupants,—from the fœcal remains which are commonly retained in the rooms,—and from the accumulations of decomposing refuse which nearly universally abound. It is still further defiled by the products of combustion. In numerous instances, I found the air in the rooms of the poor, for instance, in Alfred-row, Beckford-row, Elizabeth-place, Collingwood-place, &c., so saturated with putrescent exhalations, that to breathe it was to inhale a dangerous, perhaps fatal, poison. Already some tables have been given of the time at which death, it is presumed, would take place were there no change of the atmosphere in the rooms of the houses of some of the poor. Further illustrations are given by my friend Mr. Taylor, in the First Report of the Metropolitan Sanitary Commission.

To accomplish ventilation it is necessary that the air from without should be pure. Effective drainage, cleansing, and prevention of nuisances must *precede* all attempts to secure perfect ventilation. Examples abound where the inmates prefer the stench from within, to the stench from without; and it is a question, whether the free admission of air, loaded with emanations from drains, and cesspools, and decomposing refuse, is not much more dangerous than the continued and repeated respiration of the same air. Numerous cases of disease attest the impropriety of ventilating rooms by apertures which admit air loaded with impurities.

Wherever the greatest destitution is prevalent, there likewise ventilation is most defective. An insufficient supply of food renders the system less capable of bearing those changes of temperature, and currents of air, which would otherwise be agreeable. Protection from cold, therefore, becomes an especial primary object with the poor. They economise their fuel in their management and application of it, so that the air shall impinge gently upon their persons; and this management becomes the more marked, as the means of the inmates are reduced. This practical management of fuel extends to those rich persons whose bodies, enfeebled by disease, inertion, or a foul atmosphere, are placed in the same position as if they had suffered from a scanty supply of food.

The greatest importance is to be attached to the respiration of pure air. This will be the more readily acknowledged when we recollect that we breathe 28,000 times in one day and night. After those sanitary arrangements, therefore, which secure a pure atmosphere, the greatest benefits may be expected to flow from those great improvements which shall provide for every apartment an independent ingress for fresh air, and an egress for vitiated air, which, though small, shall be in constant operation, and capable of regulation.

It is true, that such an arrangement may not be so perfect as machinery, furnaces, and showers of water may command, and that it may be somewhat deranged by the action of high winds; but it will not induce severe draughts, the great and almost insurmountable objection of the poor; and it will remove an enormous and most oppressive evil—an evil which not only enfeebles a vast proportion of our town population, especially the poor weavers, but which likewise induces much disease, and destruction of life. This is the result which society is most interested in bringing about.

VENTILATION OF PUBLIC BUILDINGS.

The only public buildings in Bethnal-green are churches and schools; they present the most defective arrangements with regard to warming and ventilating. Some of the churches have galleries near the ceiling, with most defective arrangements for the egress of the vitiated air; others, again, have no arrangements whatever, either for the admission of pure air, or the egress of foul air. The occupants of the galleries necessarily suffer, either from a highly vitiated atmosphere, or from violent currents of cold air, when the windows behind them are opened. In some churches the arrangements for warming are conducted with the same perfect and profound ignorance of the laws of heat, as of ventilation. (In one of them e.g. an enormous open stove, like a cast-iron furnace, is situate in the middle of the centre aisle. It broils those near by its radiating heat, while the strong currents of air, required to feed it, chill those at a little distance.) This state of things is the more to be regretted, as few places so readily admit of improvements in ventilation as churches. No improvements, however, are to be anticipated, till a qualified person shall point out the defective state of churches as to ventilation, and shall *require* the execution of those simple and effective alterations which are so greatly needed for the comfort and health of the worshippers. It is to be remembered, that twenty-four gallons of noxious fluid are given off from the lungs and skins of 1,000 persons during the two hours that Divine Service occupies.

The ventilation and warming of the greater number of the schools in this parish are most defective, and urgently require efficient superintendence. The following remarks from Dr. Reid are so extremely apposite as to deserve introduction here:—" If any buildings should be subjected to inspection, in reference to their arrangements for ventilation, school-rooms pre-eminently present themselves for consideration, not only from the powerful effect which ventilation must have upon the health of pupils, but also from the influence which the maintenance of a pure atmosphere, *and from the example of the simple manner in which it may be sustained*, must exert in disseminating widely throughout the whole community a practical knowledge of means that are equally applicable to the habitations of the higher classes and the dwellings of the poor." Whatever liberty be given to builders to construct, and to masters to employ workmen in, and to inhabitants to occupy, dwellings unfit to preserve and maintain health. It would be a most unpardonable neglect in any government preparing measures to preserve the health of the people, to omit some efficient means of controlling the ventilation of public buildings, more especially places of public worship, and instruction. When it is recollected that in churches, from their generally ill-contrived means of warming and ventilating, much disease is produced, and thousands have their coughs, and colds, and trifling illnesses converted into serious maladies, and sometimes fatal diseases, and that the general dread of the inconvenience likely to result from a two hours' exposure to agencies so dangerous and distressing as cold, and damp on the one hand, and a hot and foul air on the other, prevents numbers of weakly and indisposed persons from availing themselves of the benefits of public worship; and when, in addition, it is known that of all the sources of injury to the health of the young, none is more powerful than foul air, and that the chief cause of the excessive prevalence of scofula among children is to be found in the constant respiration of the same air; the exemption of such places of public resort from a just, and beneficent supervision, and control becomes almost criminal. It cannot be sufficiently impressed on authorities, teachers, and individuals, that in two hours, the period usually continuously devoted to divine service, and to education, more than four hogsheads of pure air are required for each person, in order to convert 900 pints of blood into a state fit to sustain life, and that every individual is constantly pouring forth with his breath a poison, which, supposing he occupied a room ten feet square, that is containing 1000 cubic feet of air, would at the low estimate of sixteen respirations in a minute, produce death in twenty-four hours. But, when we find six and seven, and in some instances, eight or nine persons occupying a room six feet and a-half high, by nine feet and a-half broad, and deep, the ordinary size of the rooms in which the poor families of Bethnal-green live, and this space still further encroached upon by tables, chairs, beds, furniture, and litter, and the bodies of the occupants themselves, 500 cubic feet of air, alone, in the latter case, at the utmost, will be found to remain to supply the vital demands of the family, and hence, that sleep, occupying seven hours, will, with these persons, produce seventeen and a-half times as much poisonous gas as would, in the case of the single individual occupying a room ten feet square, have sufficed to produce death; what wonder then, that unhealthy bodies, and weak minds, stunted growth, impaired strength, scrofula, consumption, and other ills that flesh is *not* heir to, should devastate so miserable a population, so violently outraging the natural laws. And, yet, deploring such inevitable, but most common results, how can a government omit the subject of the ventilation of the present existing public buildings and schools, and submit, without a strong effort, its adult population during four or six hours a week, the period occupied in divine service, and also, an immense proportion of its young, for thirty hours a week, the average period occupied in the education of the young, to causes of disease the same, and nearly as powerful as those thus fearfully illustrated.

All the clergymen with whom I have spoken, and all teachers, and those interested in the education of the young, have universally manifested a great desire for enlightenment on the subjects of warming and ventilation, and no boon would be received by them with more thankfulness than an improvement on the present ignorant and pernicious system. In none of the churches, schools, or places of public resort in Bethnal-green, does it seem to be at all understood, that combustion produces foul air, for no attempts, except in St. Matthew's Church, and there only partially, are made to get rid of the products. This is not to be wondered at, for nowhere, almost in this parish, is it apparently known that a candle is as injurious as a human being in deteriorating the air, or that two fourteen-hole Argand burners consume as much air as eleven men.

The better to illustrate the necessity of supervision, to improve the sanitary condition of schools, those attached to St. Matthew's and St. James-the-Less may be selected. The St. Matthew schools, consist of the Charity, National, and Infant Schools, they were built in 1846, and consist of two large rooms, for scholastic purposes; there are other rooms, for other purposes. The building is situate in the north western corner of the church-yard, which is filled to repletion with corpses, the underground portion of the building consists of a central passage 49 feet long, and a side entrance. This passage is branched with seventeen brick vaults, or low cellars, which are used as catacombs, four of these are public cellars, in these last I counted ninety-six coffins piled one on the other, like so many bales of goods. I could not ascertain the number of bodies deposited in the other vaults, one only of which was bricked up. There is a large aperture at the end of the passage, for the emission of air from this place, the aperture is right under, and close to, the back entrance to the school, as well as to a most abominably filthy privy used by the children. On endeavouring to examine the state of this place, I was overcome by the most distressing nausea I have ever experienced during my sanitary investigations; whether this nausea should be entirely attributed to the filthy cesspool, or was partly due to the escape of foul air from the catacombs, I did not stay to inquire. I presume, however, that it was chiefly attributable to the former cause. How the children can use, and remain in, such a place, is almost incomprehensible.

There is no supply of water whatever for the wants of the children, and the warming is accomplished by a common stove in the centre of the room, utterly insufficient to diffuse either an equable, or a sufficient heat; the children must therefore suffer greatly during winter from cold. The upper room is 75 feet long, by 32 and a-half broad, at the sides the walls are ten feet four inches high, but the roof, being triangular, reaches in the centre a height of twenty-two feet six inches. Allowing nothing for the cross beams, desks, and raised platform, the bodies of the children, &c., this room contains 40·037 cubic feet of air. It is occupied from nine a.m. till twelve noon, and from two till four p.m. by, on an average, 275 boys and the master. This number of persons, in the three hours of morning teaching, calculating eighteen inspirations to the minute, and twenty cubic inches of air to each respiration, generate 398 cubic feet of carbonic acid gas, or foul air, exactly one part in 100 of the whole contents of the room; consequently, unless there be some provision for the egress of the foul air, and the admission of pure air, the usual consequences arising from the respiration of a poisonous atmosphere, must be produced:—as wherever the proportion of carbonic acid gas is increased from scarcely one part in a thousand, the natural proportion of carbonic acid gas in the atmosphere, to one part in one hundred, its deleterious effects begin to be obviously manifested in man, by headache, languor, general oppression, and more or less stupor; these are the obvious and immediate effects. But, besides the foul air generated in the room itself, the children have the air they breathe still further contaminated by the hot and foul air which ascends by a staircase, from the lower school-room, and which will be presently spoken of: moreover, during the three hours of teaching, they have poured out from their lungs and skins in the form of vapour, nearly fifty-two pints of noxious fluid; which noxious fluid is held in solution in the air, and still further defiles and contaminates it. Now the only means of ventilation, and of getting rid of this great amount of poisonous air, consist in opening the small windows on either side, and even this can scarcely be done except during the periods when the room is not used, but if the windows on the south side be opened, an atmosphere loaded with grave-yard emanations sweeps into the room, if on the north side, a nearly as bad result follows, for, but a short time since, a slaughter-house where a great number of cattle were usually killed, is close bye, and though the slaughtering has ceased, still foul smells, and most offensive effluvia arise; it will not then, under these circumstances, be deemed a matter of surprise, that the children constantly suffer from headache and sickness, from languor and listlessness, that they doze and are inattentive, and that fainting and vomiting is a nearly daily occurrence. The master and pupils alike complain of the most distressing sensations, from this wholesale respiration of foul air, which they themselves term very offensive.

The lower room is forty-nine feet long, thirty-four and a-half broad, and eleven feet 4 inches high; it consequently contains 19.018 cubic feet of air: this space is encroached upon by a staircase, benches, the bodies of the children, &c. In this room, on an average, 135 girls are taught for the periods already specified. They and the mistress consequently generate 196 cubic feet of carbonic acid gas during the matinal hours; a quantity in the proportion of one part in every ninety-seven of the aerial contents of the room. A proportion sufficient to produce sensations and effects even more distressing and deleterious than those above referred to, but there is likewise poured out from the lungs and skins of the children during the same period, more than twenty-five pints of noxious fluid which is held in solution in the air they breathe.

Between the morning and afternoon hours the windows are generally opened to procure ventilation, but it has always been found that by four o'clock the sense of heat and oppression has become as marked as at noon, thus proving that a considerable quantity of foul air is present, when afternoon teaching begins.

The day school attached to the church of St. James-the-Less consists of the upper room of a cottage, built in 1843; the size of the room is 27 feet in length by 15 feet in breadth and 10 feet in height; from 70 to 120 children are there daily taught for the periods specified, supposing the average attendance to be 95; these 95 children, excluding the master, would require 3,568 cubic feet of perfectly pure air to be supplied to them during the three hours, but the room itself only contains 4,050 cubic feet of air, and during these three hours 137 cubic feet of carbonic acid gas are produced by respiration, or one part in twenty-nine and a fraction of the atmosphere of the room, and if the space occupied by the bodies of the children were deducted from the aerial contents of the room, the proportion would be still more frightful. Moreover, during the same three hours there are thrown out from the skins and lungs of the children nearly 18 pints of noxious fluid, which intermingles with and remains in solution in the air.

Although no complaints are made as to the general health of the children, yet when the attendance is great, it is stated by Mr. M'Rae, the Master, that the heat has been *most oppressive*, notwithstanding the whole of the four windows in the room were opened. As this oppressive heat is, in reality, not a sensation arising from simple elevation of temperature, but from the respiration of impure air, and the impossibility of excreting the carbonic acid gas which has been formed within the body, it is sufficient to indicate that foul air accumulates to such an extent as to exert a depressing effect on the various organs of the body, and a most injurious influence upon the health of the young.

HOUSE CLEANSING BY DRAINAGE AND REMOVAL OF REFUSE, BY DRAINAGE.

" Among the evils which appear to operate with the greatest severity on the condition of all, and especially on the labouring classes, are those arising from the absence of a proper attention to drainage. They prevail almost universally, to an extent altogether incompatible with the maintenance of the public health." (Second Report Com. Health of Towns.)

House drainage is nearly entirely awanting in Bethnal-green; except in a *very small number* of cases, the houses, when they are provided with drains, drain only into cesspools; the number that drain into sewers is very small indeed. An immense number of the houses of the poorer sorts, and nearly all those in gardens, are unprovided with drains of any kind. The inhabitants, therefore, are compelled to get rid of their fluid refuse, by throwing it on the gardens, yards, or streets. Sometimes holes are dug in the gardens, or yards, to receive the refuse water. These holes are frequently closely adjacent to the wells whence the occupants derive their supply of water.

Three years ago, 1,000 yards of sewer were made from Pollard's-row to Shoreditch Church, yet not a dozen houses have formed any connexion with it. This fact sufficiently proves that it is necessary to make it compulsory on owners of houses to form drains in connexion with houses.

A great number of the courts and alleys are altogether unprovided with house-drains, or where they do exist, they are mere surface-drains, and are nearly always choked up, and thus become great nuisances. A great portion of the disease in the parish is to be found occurring in these filthy, undrained courts and alleys.

It is the more essential that house-drainage should be perfect, inasmuch as the houses and streets in this parish have generally been built without any regard to levels; when the streets and footpaths, therefore, are properly made and levelled, the houses are frequently placed below the level of the streets, and thus become excessively damp. Numbers of houses were observed to be so much below the level of the neighbouring streets, that the ground-floors greatly resembled under ground cellars, and were, really, and truly, in a state, both as regarded light and dryness, incompatible with healthy existence; and yet these are the houses which generally are altogether unprovided with house-drainage.

It is unnecessary to enter very fully into the economical arrangements of house-drainage; these have been fully exemplified in the First Report of the Metropolitan Sanitary Commission. It may, however, be necessary, in order to prove the general want of house drainage, to advert to some of the facts with regard to the drainage under the late Sewer Commission: Mr. Beek, the surveyor, has stated that instances of 2,000 or 3,000 feet of sewerage have been carried out and not half a dozen communications made; that the late commission was not in the habit of draining courts and alleys, but of introducing sewers in that situation; that such sewers were of half-a-brick, 3 feet 6 inches by 2 feet 3 inches in size; and that the expense of building it is under 6s. a-foot, but that he would estimate it at 7s. or 8s.

Alderman Musgrove has given evidence to the following effect, which, to ensure perspicuity and brevity, I have put in a tabular form.

TOWER HAMLETS COMMISSION OF SEWERS.

Extension of Sewerage.		Persons communicating with the additional Sewers.	Entire communications throughout the District that year.
In the year	Feet.		
1838	5·555	2	31
1839	2·137	27	80
1840	8·577	50	84
1841	13·841	58	110
1842	5·541	103	152
1843	4·054	70	122
1844	3·587	54	104
1845	13·402	96	140
1846	6·522	125	178
1847	13·176	165	182
In 10 years.	76·386	750	1,183

It thus appears that of every 100 feet of extension of sewerage one person only was found to avail himself of the work, and throughout the whole districts there was only one communication in every sixty-four and a-half feet. When the nearly utter want of sewerage shall be exemplified, the wretchedly defective state of the houses in Bethnal-green, as regards house drainage, must be most obvious.

In consequence of the want of efficient sewerage, and of the drains, now in common use, passing through the property of various persons, it continually happens that the greatest difficulties arise in keeping them clean, however free the drain from a house may be; if, at its extremity, or in its course, it is dilapidated, or blocked up, where, in another person's ground, it becomes a source of never ending annoyance, and expence, and a great nuisance. I have twice in the course of 6 years, been compelled, at considerable expense, to open through its whole extent and cleanse the private drain leading from my house, while the real cause of the obstruction was at a considerable distance, and in another person's property. Moreover, the like expense was lately entailed on my neighbour. Already, in New Tyssen St. 58, and Garden Place 59, District No. 4, are exemplified the evil results of such abominations as filthy and choked drains.

A further illustration of these evils is afforded in the fact, that of four houses in Elizabeth Street, Hackney Road, namely, No. 5. 6. 7. and 8. three have a drain under the floor, constantly emitting the most offensive smells, and that the bad results which thence arise might be avoided if the landlord of the corner house would permit a drain to be carried across his back premises;—whereas he will not allow one already existing, belonging to No. 9, to be cleansed out. My informant states he is prepared to prove, that the families occupying these houses are far from well, that one, in particular, has frequently been visited with fevers, and illness, during the last six years, and that the mother and eldest child, have died in consequence; that the smells were so intolerable that the doors and windows required to be frequently opened, and that the walls are soaked with the damp from the drains, to the height of several feet; the children slept in the ground room. At No. 8 two of one of the families living there, have been laid up for months with ague and fever; and I have constantly observed in some of the houses close by, in the main road, renting at 40*l.* a year, effluvia dangerous to the health, arising from foul drains.

Some powers, then, to prevent private drains, through no fault of the occupiers, becoming pestilential nuisances are obviously required, and must form a part of any efficient Sanitary Bill.

BY REMOVAL OF REFUSE.

"Filth and the absence of facilities for its removal depress the energies and engender disease and death." " The great moral results consequent upon an increase in the means of cleanliness, have not yet received the attention which their importance merits; the domestic comfort of a poor man's abode, and his own self-respect, are mainly dependent upon this." (Second Rep. Com. Health of Towns.)

The importance of a ready and efficient means to get rid of the more solid refuse from houses is second only to efficient sewerage and drainage. No person accustomed to the common decencies of civilisation, can have any conception of the amount of filth usually in, and surrounding the poor man's dwelling, unless indeed he has gone into their houses and inspected their small and dirty yards. The exterior appearances of the streets, inhabited by the poor, may, perchance, through the operation of paving and scavenging appear tolerably cleanly, but in scarcely any instance, when the houses themselves are visited, and the yards inspected, are not collections of all kinds of refuse, garbage, ashes, dirt, decomposing cabbage leaves, and other offensive vegetable remains, oftentimes dung, and sometimes putrescent animal remains, to be found either abundantly distributed over the surface of the dirty yard, or piled into a heap in a corner. In either case the heap is exposed to the action of the rain which soaks into it, hastens decomposition, dissolves the putrescent, fœtid matter, washes it over the surface of the yard, and causes it to form an intimate union with the soil. Truly does such a soil sow the seeds of disease and death, every rain which falls augments the quantity and power of the poison, every sun that shines raises a vapour charged with deadly poison. It is the general practice to condemn the poor for the filthy state of their dwellings, in sweeping accusations that, "the poor are naturally dirty;" that, " they love dirt," " and would not, if they could, be clean." Before replying to these accusations, let us ascertain what means the poor possess to get rid of their solid refuse. The parish contracts with a dust-man, from whom at present it receive 60*l.* per annum, to remove from the houses (excluding private property,) all collections of ashes; the contractor is *nominally* bound to go into the back yards of the houses, and remove thence the collection, he is likewise bound to remove all refuse, in the general use of the word, dust heaps, or rather heaps of ashes. The times at which the contractor's cart goes round is not certain, no provision, therefore, can be made to have the refuse in readiness for him. In name, he is bound *on complaint* to remove collections of ashes, &c., *but in practice it is not so.* Practically, therefore, the dust and garbage heaps of the poor must either remain on their premises, or they must themselves remove them. But they can only remove them from the yards to the streets: *there* then the refuse is deposited to rot and to putrify, and mingle with the dust and mud, and to be scattered on the pavement, and to defile the passengers. The filthy streets remain uncleansed till their foulness startles the eye of the scavenging department. During all this period, whether the refuse be on the premises, where it is continually accumulating, or on the streets, it is giving off vapours loaded with unhealthy emanations. Wherever I went, I found the most loud and bitter complaints against the dust contractor, for the filthy state in which the inhabitants were compelled to remain, in consequence of his never, or very rarely, removing their dust heaps. These complaints in many places assumed the tone of the deepest indignation, and evidently arose from an earnest conviction of a great outrage being committed upon them, and of a cruel negligence or indifference to their wants and necessities, actuating the authorities. "The people never die here, they are murdered by the fever," was the exclamation of one inhabitant in Half Nichol-street. I could not deny the assertion; the state of the back yards, and the state of the street, were enough to breed and nourish, and mature a pestilence. Truly, indeed, are such convictions at the bottom of much discontent, truly do they endanger the fabric of society, and the danger is the greater, as the convictions are founded on truth and bitter experience. It is impossible but that habits of cleanliness, decency and self-respect, must be sacrificed by the condition of things which at present exists with regard to house cleansing by drainage, and the removal of refuse. It is impossible but that discontent, and disputes should arise, and that working-men, finding their homes made wretched and uncomfortable, and surrounded with nuisances, should leave them for the public-house, there to learn, and soon to indulge in, habits of intemperance, which indulgence soon leads to vicious propensities which, in their turn, give rise to a large class of crimes. It is perfectly true, that, on analysis, numbers of crimes are clearly traceable to the low state of physical comforts of the poor, to the filth which surrounds their dwellings, and to the absence of facilities for its removal; these agencies depress the energies, and lead to intemperance through the desire to impart false strength to a debilitated physical and nervous system, to a disregard to all moral and social ties, to disease and premature decay. From my personal investigations into the state of the dwellings of the poor, I am more and more convinced that the sum of wretchedness, of misery, of destitution, of slow corroding care, of wasting disease, and early death, which they endure through a neglect of cleanliness—a neglect cruelly attributed to them, but which might be thrown back as a bitter taunt to those who really cause it, namely the middle and upper classes,—forms a most serious charge for which these last are answerable to Him who placed them in their various positions in society. As a people we deserve to be visited with pestilence, it we longer neglect the great social duties which we owe to the poorer classes congregated in our towns.

PRIVIES AND CESSPOOLS.

".The deficient number of privies in the poorer quarters of towns, and the large number of inhabitants resorting to them, deprives them of any right to be considered private, and render it absolutely necessary for the safety of the public health, that some alteration should be made in the law regarding them."
—(Second Rep. Com. Health of Towns.)

It is scarcely possible to conceive the utter degradation of the human mind which permits it, at least, to tolerate the disgusting offensiveness of these abominable nuisances, which exist in the form of common privies, in the poorer neighbourhoods. One open necessary for numerous families, and for 20, 30, or 50 persons, is surely most objectionable, but it is quite a common occurrence. It is true that Bethnal-green is not so bad as Sunderland, where there is only one necessary for every 76 persons, but there is a vast amount of moral degradation entailed upon the inhabitants by their being compelled to make use of such a scanty number of such filthy receptacles.

In the preceding tables the condition of the privies, so far as I could learn, was given, but it must by no means be inferred that those places which have not p.f. attached to them do not deserve the characteristic letters. This is the only part of the table which is incomplete.

The generality of the privies in this parish are full, and most offensive, great numbers are overflowing. The cesspools attached are, in the majority of instances, in no better condition. Many of the privies are wooden sheds erected over holes from which a surface hollow conducts off the fluid refuse to some other part of the ground. Many are most dilapidated, and some are dangerous to make use of. In numerous instances the soil has infiltrated the walls, percolated through them, and spread itself over the surface of the neighbouring yard; the soil has likewise percolated through the walls, and into the houses, and in some instances, the floors have been saturated, and have been rendered very quagmires of filth; the flooring, in such cases, has become rotten. In numerous instances, the inhabitants have piled either in their yards, or in their houses, or in the alleys fronting the houses, collections of dust and cinders, to conceal from the eye the soil which has oozed from the neighbouring privies or cesspools.

The soil from the privies and cesspools is very rarely removed, it is an expensive process, and its occurrence is reckoned on as a disgusting event, necessary to be postponed as long as possible. The landlords of the poorer tenements very rarely indeed remove the contents of the cesspools or privies, and often neglect to do so, till compelled by the devastations which the exhalations from the soil produce, in the form of fever, and alarmed lest their property should get a bad name, and be thus rendered untenantable. The poor, left to rot in their filth, sometimes attempt to rid themselves of this nuisance, and fancy they effect it by burying the soil in their yards. Not unfrequently it happens that the supply of water to such houses is by a well in these yards; the water necessarily becomes tainted, and a slow or active poison according to the amount of soil which has percolated into it; the poor inhabitants who have gardens near or attached to their dwellings, generally manure the ground with the soil from their privies. Not only do the poor find the removal of night soil an expensive process but even those inhabiting the better class of houses and public institutions are known to remove the soil from their privies and bury it in their gardens. Often this burying consists in merely sprinkling earth over the surface of the soil so as to conceal it from sight. In some parts of the parish the privies of whole rows of houses drain into black ditches, and thus render these ditches horrible nuisances; the effects of such modes of dealing with animal refuse are daily exemplified,—head-ache, indigestion, nausea, loss of appetite, debility, pallor, wasting, diarrhœa, dysentery, cholera, fever and zymotic diseases, in a malignant form, are the every day consequences, and whenever an epidemic attacks a place, those localities, where such abominations exist, suffer the most; the influenza in Bethnal-green has chiefly exhausted its virulence in prostrating and destroying the unfortunate inhabitants of such filthy abodes. While there has been little increase in the usual mortality in the healthy, and clean streets, the mortality has been quintupled in the unhealthy and dirty streets. These dwellings are indeed reservoirs of pestilence, that only require the match to be applied to cause enormous destruction of life. In some places, as in Shacklewell-street, food cannot be retained a single night without becoming tainted, and leather rapidly becomes covered with green mould.

The disgusting and abominable state of the open and common privies, proves a source of much disease and domestic discomfort in another way; women and children find these places so repulsive that they avoid them, and retain, in their ill-ventilated rooms, their refuse; the utensils are seldom emptied on account of the trouble thereby occasioned; the air of the rooms, therefore, becomes most offensive, and deleterious, and the walls absorb the emanations, and render the abode permanently unhealthy.

The nearly total want of efficient house drainage, and the general absence of sewers, necessitate, to some extent, the present state of things. This is proved by the fact that in the *new buildings* in Hackney-road, duly provided with house drainage, water closets are attached. Probably there are more water-closets to these few houses than in all the 13,000 houses in the parish. Certainly there are not fifty water-closets for the 82,000 inhabitants.

The present customary method of emptying cesspools and privies by hand labour, and removing the soil by cartage, is excessively offensive, and occasionally the cause of serious accidents. The expense, moreover of the removal of the soil in this way, acts as an insurmountable obstacle to the riddance of this pestilential refuse from the dwellings of the poor. When it is considered that the usual cost of cleansing cesspools in London, is 1l. each time, and that the rents of the dwellings of the poor range from 1s. to 3s. 6d. and 5s. a week., it it can readily be understood, that the poor cannot cleanse their cesspools and privies, and that the landlords consider the expense very oppressive, and consequently neglect the operation. In the evidence of Mr. Beek before the metropolitan Sanitary Commission some contradictory evidence is given, to the effect that the expense of emptying the cess-pools of common tenements varies, probably, from 7s. to 10s.; but that if the man who does the work is allowed to come to the house and charge, he will charge perhaps four or five times that amount. He states, likewise, the average cost of cleansing to amount to 15s. but that that is not allowing the nightman to use his own discretion about it. It is, therefore, clear that the average as stated by the nightmen themselves, of £1 is more near the truth. But besides the expense, the offensiveness of the operation causes the process to be much neglected. Science, certainly, has made rapid progress in presenting us with chloride of manganese. A waste product of the manufacture of chlorine; procured in very large quantities (probably 160 tons a day,) and at present applied to no useful process, and consequently very cheap. This agent almost immediately destroys the disgusting odour of night soil and other animal substances in a state of putrecence, even when used in very small quantities, such as a pint to about a ton, in winter; and would consequently remove two difficulties in the way of riddance of the soil by the process of hand labour and cartage, namely: the offensiveness and the danger. But when conjoined with the new method of flushing and cleansing cesspools by means of the common fire engine and hose, the remaining difficulty, namely—the expense is surmounted, the expense is only one-sixth that of the old process.

PAVING.

The surfaces of the streets, and their proper inclinations for the speedy removal of surface water, are sadly neglected in many parts of this parish. Many of the streets are in the worst condition possible, without any pavement, or harder substance for their protection, than what the natural soil affords. In this condition, they have long remained, with gradually increasing inequalities on the surface, which form basins, not only for the reception of the rain and refuse water, but for the refuse from the adjoining houses which the occupants invariably distribute on the streets. Pleasant-row in the Green district, affords an example of the *ne plus ultra* of street abomination. Within the last 10 years the greatest change has taken place in many of the streets of Bethnal Green; places which were formerly in a state indicating the most disgraceful neglect, and characteristic of the most primitive barbarism, have been paved and converted, so far as paving without efficient drainage can convert such places, into comparatively clean and pleasant roadways. It is now possible to pass along the chief roadways without unusual personal uncleanness, but nearly all the byeways are still deplorably filthy. With about two or three exceptions, all the courts of this parish are unpaved.

STREET CLEANSING.

"The effect which a due attention to this important branch of the good government of towns may produce on the physical condition of a population is second only to sewerage."—Dr. Arnott.

There are sixty Commissioners appointed to superintend the paving, lighting, cleansing, and improving the parish. The facts with regard to the cleansing afford satisfactory proof, either that the commissioners *cannot* sufficiently cleanse the parish, that they will not, or know not how to do the work.

Undoubtedly they deserve commendation for the efforts they have made to pave the streets, and for the great improvements which they have effected during the last ten years; much, however, still remains for them to do.

But the shamefully negligent way in which they superintend the cleansing of the parish, sadly derogates from the praise due to them for their paving efforts. On account of the high charge of the contractors for cleansing the parish, the commissioners have taken that work into their own hands, and appointed their own paid agent to perform the work. The work consists in cleansing thirty-three miles of streets, and nearly one hundred miles of byeway. It is executed by thirteen decrepid old men, nine horses, and five carts, at an expense of nearly 800*l*. (it is true that about two miles or two miles and a-half of roadway are under the metropolitan commission. This part is the cleanest and best attended to in the parish.) This exposition of the means adapted to the end sought to be accomplished, is sufficient clearly to point out the utter impossibility of preserving any thing like cleanliness, especially among a people who make the streets the common reservoir and receptacle for refuse of every kind, and where the cry of "Gardez l'eau," of the olden times should be momentarily uttered. It is calculated that 1000 yards form the amount which can be effectually swept by an able-bodied scavenger in one day, now as there are thirty-three miles of streets, and 100 miles of byeways in the parish which require sweeping, they must contain 1,168,640 superficial square yards; on the assumption that none of the streets are wider than twenty-four feet, and none of the byeways wider than twelve feet;—it follows that, with the whole thirteen scavengers employed by the parish, supposing them to be all able-bodied, and all employed in scavenging, (they have the care of five carts and nine horses besides) according to this estimate of a man's labour, all the streets and bye-ways cannot be more effectively gone over than *once in ninety days*, including Sundays:—

In cleansing the streets, it is the practice to shovel the mud on the streets, into heaps by the roadside; these heaps frequently remain several days before the cart comes round to receive them. In the meantime they have been broken up and much of the mud redistributed over the road by passing vehicles. A considerable quantity of mud therefore is *never* removed from the streets. Another mode of cleansing the streets consists in brushing the fluid mud and filth from the centre of the roadway, into the gutters, and upon the paved footpath. From the nearly total absence of efficient drainage, this fluid mud remains in this position till again spread over the surface of the streets by traffic, or partly washed away by the accidental agency of heavy showers. I have also seen the muddy refuse on the streets swept to the centre of the street, but I have never seen the mud thus heaped up removed. The operation of sweeping or brushing the streets is performed in a careful manner, so as to leave the prominent parts of the stones or surface *bare*, but to *fill up* every hollow and rut with the fluid, fœtid slime. The first shower of rain renders such streets as filthy and dirty as ever. The streets which are regularly cleansed twice a week (the greatest amount of cleanliness thought necessary) are Bethnal-green-road, Brick-lane, Hare-street, and John-street. The other streets are cleansed once a fortnight, "*or as soon as they become dirty.*" The courts and alleys in this parish may, with great truth, be said to be never cleansed. In two or three instances, where there is a good water-supply and paving, the courts are, through the indefatigable exertions of the occupants, tolerably clean; but, with these exceptions, the abominably filthy state of the courts and alleys can scarcely be surpassed. The observation of the Health of Towns Commissioners peculiarly well applies to this district:—" It might have been expected," they say, " that the power with which the local authorities are invariably invested by their Local Acts had been exercised freely, as the best compensation that could be made for deficiencies in other respects. *The fact is exactly the reverse of what it ought to be.*"

The Commissioners of Cleansing seem to be unaware of the economical, as well as the other, advantages which an efficient system of scavenging produces to a community. It has been proved most satisfactorily that the *daily* cleansing of *a large city*—of its innermost courts and closes—is not unattainable on account of pecuniary expense; and that the charge upon the public amounts to about 2,000*l.* a year; and this principle is well established, that all parts of a town require cleansing *every day*, and the portions inhabited by the poor more frequently than those occupied by the rich.

For a few additional hundreds of pounds annually the parish could be effectually cleansed, and *kept clean*, in all its streets, alleys, and courts, every day.

SEWERAGE.

Bethnal-green has thirty-three miles of streets, and at least 100 miles of bye-ways, not including the length of courts and alleys, which require drainage.

The whole length of sewers which is laid down in this parish amounts to less than seven miles and three quarters (13,565 yards), of which one mile and a half and sixty yards skirt the north and south of the parish, and are as much in the adjoining parishes as in Bethnal-green. A very considerable part of this limited extent of sewerage has been recently constructed by the Woods and Forests, close by the Victoria Park, at present this extension of the sewage does not communicate with a single house. Bethnal-green-road, the main road in the parish, has no sewer (with the exception of two small patches) for 1,600 yards. Hackney-road, another main road, has no sewer for 390 yards. Cambridge-road, including Bethnal-green and the Dog-row, the next and most important road, has no sewer for 800 yards. Brick-lane, densely populated, and where there is much traffic, has no sewer for 770 yards, and would require 450 more out of the parish to communicate with the main sewer. If such be the condition of the main streets, where, hitherto, sewers have almost exclusively been laid down, it will readily be believed that the bye-ways are utterly neglected. The filthy, abominable state of the streets, courts, and alleys in Bethnal-green, is readily accounted for when the above facts are considered. The prefixed MAP of the SEWERS has been copied from that of the late Tower Hamlets commission, published in 1843, and all the additional sewerage which has been completed up to the present time has been kindly inserted for me, by Mr. Bainbridge, the surveyor of the parish. A glance at this map will demonstrate the dreadful and deplorable want of sewage, especially in the densely crowded Town district, and will explain, to a great extent, the lamentable state of the parish, as to uncleanness, sickness and mortality.

In the First Report of the Metropolitan Sanitary Commission is to be found such a mass of conclusive evidence as to the waste, ignorance, indifference, and neglect of the late Tower Hamlets Commission of Sewers, as must appal even the stoutest friend of the late Commissioners. Their doings are now matters of history, but the results of their conduct are to be found in the misery and wretchedness of thousands, and in the poor-rates at 1s. 6d. in the pound, or 30 per cent. per annum. It is possible to submit, for a short time, to the present state of things, because the new Commissioners are pledged by the history of their lives, by their reputation, and by their position and power, to ameliorate the frightful and deplorable results brought about by former ignorance, waste, and neglect. The inhabitants patiently, but most anxiously, await the change. It is of importance, however, that it should be known that the only method used by the late commission to cleanse their sewers, was to open them and remove the deposit by cartage, this they did at an annual expense of from five to six hundred pounds a year. They had sixteen outlets into the Thames, but for seven hours in every twelve, the sewers are shut up, and are mere reservoirs of filth. It is stated in the Report of the Health of London Association on the Sanitary condition of the Metropolis, that " in the district of the Tower Hamlets Commission of Sewers, there were, within the last few months upwards of 10,000 feet of open sewers, many of which were in the crowded neighbourhood of Mile-end, New-town, and Bethnal-green, and the last printed report of the Commission demonstrates, in addition to the ignorance and negligence of the Commission, as to the works executed by them, a most wasteful and extravagant expenditure in the working of the commission: for,—whereas the rate-payers had the benefit of ill-constructed, costly, and inefficient sewers bestowed on them at an expense of £7864 10s. 4d., they had £3152 5s. 4d., charged to them for working the commission. That is to say, for every £100 contributed by the rate-payers, to these irresponsible gentlemen, £28 12s. 0d. was spent in ascertaining how the other £71 6s. should be expended.

INTERMENTS.

Interments in this parish take place to a great extent, in the crowded graveyards of Shoreditch Church (which is partly in this parish), of St. Matthew, and of Gibraltar Chapel, and in the Jews' burying-ground. There are no great number of interments in either of the cemeteries in the Green District. In Shoreditch and in St. Matthew's the ground has been very considerably raised by the numerous bodies which have been interred. I regret to state, that at no very great distance of time it was the practice to burn the coffins in one of the church-yards; it would be needless to inquire what became of the corpses. It would be greatly to the credit and advantage of the Christians, if they would follow the practice of the Hebrews, who *never*, upon any account, reopen a grave, or inter more than one in it. They bury at a depth of four feet below the surface, and when the ground has been fully occupied, they cover the whole surface with a fresh layer of earth, to a height of four feet, in which they again bury as before. This process has been twice followed in the Jews' burying-ground, so that three persons are interred in every 21 feet (3 feet by 7 feet), at a depth of 4, 8, and 12 feet below the surface. This practice is to be preferred to sinking a deep grave, as is the custom in some grave-yards, burying in it, filling it up a few feet, and leaving the grave open for the next occupant, when the same process is carried on, till the last coffin reaches a few feet sometimes a few inches from the surface.

The practice of the Hebrews proves that interment in towns is not *necessarily* accompanied with desecration of the dead. It is the practice in St. Matthew's to bury in vaults, in the church, and as lately as last week a body was thus deposited. This practice is most abominable and reprehensible, and imperiously demands immediate abatement, as an offensive, dangerous, and disgusting nuisance. The smells and exhalations from a dead body are quite as offensive, and deleterious, as those from a dead ox or horse. Yet vaults, and grave-yards are less thought of than knackers'-yards, and slaughter-houses, which probably will be removed long before attention shall be bestowed on the evil effects which arise from neglecting to provide appropriate places for the decomposition of the remains of the human species. *Proh pudor.*

It is earnestly desired that the whole subject of interment in towns should receive the early attention of Parliament, and that the practice should be abolished.

The following Table represents the present state of the Grave-yards and Cemeteries in this parish:—

	When opened	Area	How much used	Number interred last Year in the Ground	In Vaults	Total Number interred last Year	Total Number interred	Soil	Lowest Depth of Graves	Depth below Surface at which cease to bury	Number buried in One Grave	Space to each Grave	Average Number of Burials per Acre
Graveyards in connexion with Churches.													
St. Matthew	1746	12,100 sq.yd	5-6th	765	35	800	50,000	light earth, gravel below	24 feet	3 feet	sometimes 12	.....	240
St. Peter	1841	70f. by 70 f.	....	21	none	21	78	do.	14 feet	7 feet	3	7f. by 3 usual	.....
St. James-the-Less	1846	1 acre	1 grave	1	none	1	1	clay, gravel, sand	7 feet	none specid.	1, till ground gone over	.....	.....
St. Bartholomew	1844	....	1-10 or 1-12	51	none	51	114	rub. gravl, clay dry	12 feet	8 feet	.....	6½ by 2½ as close as can pack	181
Shoreditch	1740	8000 sq. yds	nearly all	712	12	724	probably 75,000	.....	20 feet	5 feet	as many as can be packed in 15 ft. deep.	.....	.....
Chapels.													
Gibraltar	....	....	a large prton not at all	.....	.....	.....	.....	light veget. clay gravel	20 or 21 f.	4 feet	depends on capacity.	accord-ing to circum-stances	†
Providence	....	....											
Victoria Pk Cem.*													
N.E. London Cem.*													
Cemeteries.													
Of Great Synagogue	1796	3 & 4 acres	2-3rds	210	none	210	7,000	.....	7 feet	4f. 6	only 1	7f. by 3	40 ‡
Of Lesser Synagogue	....	2400 sq. yds											

* These two Cemeteries have not been much used; the interments are conducted with every propriety, and I am not aware of any circumstance, in reference to them, which deserves notice, as affecting the health of the inhabitants in their immediate neighbourhood.

† The water from a very deep well, situated in the garden close by, coming out of chalk, is considered the best in the neighbourhood, and is much in request.

‡ No grave contains more than one body, and after one has been interred, the ground is never re-opened on any pretence whatsoever.

It is exceedingly curious, and not a little indicative of the very slight progress which has been made during the last half century, in the practical and scientific means of averting disease and improving the health of communities, that in the First Report of the Board of Health, dated 30th April, 1845, entitled "An Outline of a Plan to Prevent the Spreading of the Plague, or other Contagious Diseases, &c." Page 11, it is stated that "It becomes a Duty of the Magistrates likewise to appoint Burial-grounds," and "the bodies ought to be deposited at a depth of not less than six feet below the surface." Whereas, under Lord Morpeth's present Health of Towns' Bill, a depth of thirty inches has been considered sufficient to prevent the escape of the pestilential gases which arise from the putrefaction of the bodies of the human species. This retrograde movement is of the most discreditable kind, and betokens either the greatest indifference to the facts which have been so long prominently before the public, with regard to the horrid and pestilential state of the intramural burial grounds, or the greatest subservience to existing interests.

NUISANCES.

The nuisances arising from foul streets, filthy privies and cesspools, and collections of garbage, &c., in the dwellings of the poor have already been adverted to. The nuisances which are most prominent in the parish are, the nightmen's yards in Digby-street, in Turk-street, Tyssen-street, and by the canal, near Ann's-place. These abominable and disgraceful nuisances have been described. The other nuisances are smaller dustmen's yards in James-street, and some other parts of the parish, the filthy, pestilential lake in Lamb's-fields; the filthy pond, called Wellington-pond, behind St. Peter's Church; the large lake behind Ann's-place; the black ditches parallel with arch 89 of the railway, and behind Ion-square, and covering the low grounds opposite the canal, close by Chapman's-gardens—vacant spaces where refuse, garbage, and filth of all kinds are deposited such as the triangular hollow at the foot of Mape Street; the large undrained vacant space opposite Crabtree-row, covering an area of at least five acres, and formed by the erasement of a vast number of the most vile and abominable of wretched dwellings, greatly below the level of the surrounding neighbourhood, a marsh, in wet weather, and a resort for all the idle, the abandoned, and the vagabonds of the neighbourhood, the vacant space opposite Teale Street, and the passage beneath the archway near the railway terminus, &c., all these have been described in the preceding sketches. The occupations which give rise to nuisances are Ragmens yards, such as those in Bethnal Green-road, Contractor's yards, as in Rook's Place, Dairies, such as those in Cambridge Road, and in Strout-place, which is greatly complained of, and in numerous other places; pig styes which abound everywhere, and collections of dung and manure such as those in Pleasant-Place, and in Thomas-place; slaughter-houses which are scattered all over the parish, and most abound in the most densely populated districts. The slaughter-house in Mount-square, has been shown to have been exceedingly deleterious to health. Besides these, there are many other offensive and noxious occupations carried on, such as the preparing, in different ways, and for various purposes of the intestines of animals; the boiling of tripe, and the preparation of cats meat, the melting of tallow, especially the remelting of the "dabs," &c.

The most injurious occupations to the workmen which are carried on are a Lead Manufactory in Hollybush Gardens, and Lucifer Match making. I have no particulars of the true amount of disease produced by the former, but am aware of numerous cases of disease arising from the latter, which shall be elsewhere taken notice of.

It is absolutely incumbent on the commissioners for *cleansing* and improving the parish, if the wish to retain the confidence and respect of the inhabitants, that they should at once proceed to remove nearly all the forementioned nuisances, through the powers conferred upon them by Lord Morpeth's act 9 & 10, vic. It is likewise incumbent on government to regulate both the situation and the manner of conducting those industrial pursuits which are found to be deleterious to the health and lives of the workmen.

WATER SUPPLY.

The quantity of water supplied by the East London Water Company is in general good, but in wet weather the water is highly coloured, deposits much sediment, and becomes hard. The supply is, as usual, thrice weekly, and for two hours at a time, and at low pressure; the great majority of the houses are supplied with water, but, in an immense number of instances, the water is not laid on to the houses, but is supplied by a stand pipe in the yard. Frequently there is a stand pipe in the street, or alley. Sometimes, there is a stand pipe to two houses, but it is much more common to find a stand pipe supplying every three or four houses. In the courts, and alleys, and gardens there is, generally only one stand pipe to every 8, 12, 20, or even 30 houses. To many houses there is no water supply whatever, and the inhabitants require to beg it, or procure it as they best can.

The receptacles to receive the water in the better houses, are generally butts. There are very few proper cisterns. With the poor, tubs, pails, earthen jugs &c., supply the place of cisterns. A very large proportion of the poorer tenements, those, namely, where there is only one stand pipe to many houses, have no receptacles of any kind, and the inhabitants preserve water in small jugs, open pitchers or wooden vessels, in their houses, or rooms. Thorold-square, and the Crescent, Hackney Road, have pumps and sunk tanks communicating with the main. The inhabitants, therefore, have a constant supply, but in a very inconvenient mode. I found three open wooden cisterns common to many houses, the one contained the remains of fish, in a putrescent state; the wood of the second was rotten, covered with green, slimy mould, and the surface of the water iridescent from the scum floating on it; the third was an open kind of horse trough adjacent to a privy. In some instances, as in George Gardens, the barrels to receive and preserve the water are sunk in the ground, by which means the water is preserved from the deposition of dust, dirt, and ashes, &c., floating in the air, and is kept cool, but it is nearly impossible to cleanse such receptacles; and yet we have it on the authority of the Engineer to the East London, and to the Kent and Vauxhall Water Works Companies that unless the butts are cleansed once a fortnight it is impossible to preserve the water in a state of purity. In only two instances among the poorer tenements, namely in Hammonds Gardens, and in Grove-row did I find efficient butts properly situated and adapted as cisterns.

The consequences which result to the community from water being supplied to them of bad quality, are, firstly, its hardness, producing an extreme waste of soap; (the degree of hardness of the water supplied to London entails a needless expenditure of 300,000*l.* in soap, of which sum Bethnal Green bears its proportion), secondly its bad quality, creating and fostering a desire for more pleasant beverages, and thus leading to the pernicious habit of beer and spirit drinking. In Edinburgh where the water is very pure in quality, the use of beer is comparatively unknown. Unquestionably, the impurity of the water supplied to London is a very important item in the causes which produce intemperance.

The consequences of an intermittant supply of water, are, firstly, the necessity for receptacles to receive the water, and preserve a sufficiency till the next supply. This entails a very considerable expense upon the inhabitants. The cost of receptacles to London is calculated at 2,000,000*l.* which is certainly below the truth, Bethnal Green shares in this *waste*. Secondly, in the receptacles themselves deteriorating the quality of the water. The reservoirs are in very few instances efficient. Firstly, they are generally improperly placed, so that the sun's rays beat all day upon them, and thus render the water hot, and prone to putrefaction, from the vegetable matter usually held in suspension or solution. Secondly, they are, frequently, from the same cause, cleansed with great difficulty; where they are buried in the earth they can scarcely be cleansed at all :—Thirdly, the receptacles themselves are frequently rotten, and thus impart an offensive quality to the water, and hasten the decomposition of the vegetable matter in it:—Fourthly, they are generally open at the top and consequently readily receive and have deposited in them, the impurities in the atmosphere, the dust, dirt, ashes constantly floating in the air of such neighbourhoods, besides the foul matters which may be thrown into them, such as vegetable and animal remains of all kinds ;—Fifthly, from their usual proximity to the privy, (they are generally placed under one and the same roof) absorption of the poisonous exhalations which arise from the decomposition of the soil takes place, still further rendering the water unwholesome. This is an exceedingly common occurrence, I would almost say universal. When the water is taken *in doors*, which it necessarily is in all those very numerous cases where there is a common stand pipe and no receptacle, the case is still worse. Firstly, the water is exposed to a high temperature, and is thus rendered prone to decomposition ;—Secondly, it is preserved uncovered, and thus absorbs the foul, and almost pestilential gases, and exhalations which are mixed with, or suspended in the air of the close ill-ventilated rooms of the poor.

An intermittent supply, more especially as is the case in the poorer neighbourhoods where there are no receptacles to preserve it, till next supply day, necessarily curtails the *quantity* of water, renders it scarce, and important carefully to preserve the amount that is on hand. Water thus becomes stored and preserved, is niggardly applied to the common purposes of life. Firstly, it limits, and in some cases prevents house cleanliness;—secondly, it discourages personal cleanliness; water is not thrown away as useless until it has been defiled beyond using, and until it can no longer cleanse; thirdly, it prevents food being properly washed before cooking, and limits the quantity used in cooking; fourthly, it prevents the clothes being properly washed, and necessitates the same water being used repeatedly, even although foul.

The intermittent supply by stand-pipes, when there are no receptacles to receive the water, acts as a barrier to domestic and house cleansing. Firstly by entailing on the inhabitants the necessity of being present when the supply comes on, otherwise, they must lose their supply of water for two days. This necessity constantly arising, interferes seriously with the arrangements of the poor. Secondly, when there is a receptacle, the man or woman tired and overcome with the days labour dislikes, and regards as an intolerable burden, to be compelled to go to a distance, or out of doors to fetch water, it may be in the wet, or in the snow.

The supply of water, at low pressure, is likewise productive of numerous evils. Firstly, it entails upon the rich, the expense of force-pumps, if they wish water carried up to the upper floors of their houses. Secondly, it entails on the rich, who have not force pumps, and on the poor, who live on the second, third, and fourth floors of houses, the necessity of carrying up all the pure water they require, and of carrying down again all their refuse water. This heavy labour falls most oppressively on the poor, and is a grievous burden. Women and children generally suffer most. Oftentimes, the poor mother is compelled to carry a child in her arms, while she descends and ascends several flights of stairs, to procure water. When the labour is transferred to children, it often tasks their capabilities beyond their physical powers. In one instance which lately came to my knowledge, a child died from this very cause, and while in the act of carrying the burden up stairs.

The laborious task of obtaining water in this way, leads the poor to preserve their water in tubs in their rooms, and as their rooms are very small, these tubs, to be out of the way, are generally thrust below the bed, and consequently expose the water in them to certain very deleterious exhalations. Not long ago, a child, on being left by its mother in bed, was found by her, on her return, drowned in the water-tub, which had been only partly thrust below the bed.

The stand-pipes are seldom supplied with taps. When the water comes on, therefore, the water continues to flow until turned off from the main. When the courts are paved, of which I know two or three instances, this flow of water may be advantageous, as it effectually cleanses the court, and scours the drain, (when there is one,)—but, where, as in nearly all the courts, gardens and alleys, there is no paving, and the ground is altogether undefended, and where there is inefficient drainage, the flow of water becomes a great nuisance by rendering the footpaths muddy, or even quagmires, by inundating the neighbourhood, and by rendering the houses that are placed on a low level, either very damp, or positively uninhabitable.

In consequence of quarrels between the landlords of small houses, and the water company, I found numerous houses without any supply of water whatever. Shacklewell-street, for instance. The inhabitants therefore were abruptly deprived of one of the necessaries of life, from no fault of their own. They were at once plunged into great distress through causes over which they had no control, and which they were quite incompetent to remedy. The water company in cutting off the supply of water, did not punish the landlord, but the unoffending poor.

It is unnecessary here to advert to the increased security from fire, which a constant supply of water at high pressure would afford. It is necessary however to observe, that the price at which water is supplied, on the present highly objectionable plan, is excessively high, and that water, forming one of the main necessaries of life, being more important even than food, should be provided by the public, to the public; *on the most economical terms possible,* and that no principle of justice can countenance the exorbitant prices now charged for water, defective in quality, deficient in quantity, intermittent in supply, and at low pressure, when it has been abundantly proved, that a sufficient supply of pure water at a very cheap rate can readily be obtained.

The supply of water by wells is inconsiderable, still a much larger number of houses are supplied by wells, than would readily be supposed. This mode of supply, in the majority of instances, is most objectionable, inasmuch as the well derives its supply of water from fluid, which has percolated through a soil, covered, and sometimes saturated, with refuse and decomposing matter, often intimately mixed up with dung and night soil. Generally the privies and cesspools are within a few feet from such wells. In scarcely any instances are the wells sunk deep enough to get rid of surface drainage, and superficial springs. In Whisker's-gardens, some of the worst examples of such wells are to be found. There are, however two or three deep wells in the parish, which furnish a plentiful supply of good water.

SICKNESS AND DISEASE, AND MORTALITY.

Any one who has perused the facts which have been already developed in these pages must, in some measure, be prepared for the array of figures (the work of hours, and days, and weeks, but the result of which occupies but a few minutes), which tells us of the oppressive amount of sickness, and disease, and mortality unnecessarily suffered by the unfortunate poor in this parish. In the tables I shall exemplify the condition of Bethnal-green, by comparing it with that of the surrounding parishes. In the tables which have been compiled, the sickness and mortality refers to the amount occurring in the 12 months ending Oct. 1, 1847, by which means those sources of error, or exaggeration, at least, in the last quarter of 1847, which the prevalence of influenza would have given rise to, will be entirely avoided. The sickness and mortality may be taken as a fair and ordinary specimen of the unhealthiness of the parish.

It would have cost me a much greater amount of labour than I am now able to bestow to have analyzed all the diseases which have produced the mortality in this parish. I have confined my analysis to the deaths from zymotic diseases, and from all causes.

The first table which I have to present illustrates the amount of sickness and disease in the different parochial medical districts. This table is necessarily defective, as illustrating the *whole* amount of sickness and disease in the districts, because it only displays the amount attended by the parochial medical officers, altogether leaving out the cases of disease attended by dispensary medical officers, by private practitioners, or which obtain relief from hospitals. It is also defective, inasmuch as peculiar circumstances may cause one medical officer to receive many more "orders" than another; such as a character for ability, for attention, for kindness; or the reverse; such as a character for inability, for neglect, and indifference. I am not, however, aware that in any of the districts such causes at all affect the table; and as the proportion of dispensary cases, and of cases receiving relief from hospitals, as far as I can learn, is greatest in the worst districts, they may diminish the force of the facts that sickness and disease chiefly prevail in the worst districts, but do not alter the facts themselves.

It is earnestly to be desired that when highly-qualified medical officers of health shall have been appointed, some means may be taken to use, for the benefit of the public, the vast amount of information annually collected by the parochial medical officers, and which now remains undigested, and utterly useless. With a proper system of medical relief to the poor, dispensaries would be worse than useless, and out-door relief from hospitals no better. The thousands of out-door cases of disease relieved by these charities (in some measure pseudo-charities), and which are ostentatiously paraded by the governors, to show what has been done, and are put forth to procure still larger contributions, are either cases which ought properly to fall to the lot of parishes adequately to relieve and attend to, or else they are objects altogether unfit to receive public charity of any kind. By the suppression of dispensaries and out-door relief from hospitals, the whole sickness and disease of the pauper population of the parish would devolve on the parochial medical officers, and their returns would become to the statistics of disease what the returns of deaths are to the statistics of mortality. The greatest possible benefits would flow from such a grand and comprehensive system of arrangement of medical facts.

The five Districts have each very nearly the same population, but the relative amount of sickness and disease is widely different, and abundantly evidences the dismal effects arising from over-crowding, and neglected cleanliness.

TABLE OF THE NUMBER OF SICK ATTENDED BY THE PAROCHIAL MEDICAL OFFICERS IN ONE YEAR,—Ending Oct. 1, 1847, and the remuneration per case, and per visit.

TABLE I.

Parish of Bethnal Green.	Salary.	Cases attended.	Visits paid.	Rate per case.	Rate per Visit.
District No. 1.	£50	515	5361	1s. 11¼	2d. —9-10
— — 2.	50	536	3616	1 10¼ 5-10	3 ¼ 2-10
— — 3.	50	499	3781	2 0	3 —6-10
— — 4.	50	996	8537	1 0	1 ¼ 6-10
— — 5.	40	969	1823	2 11¼ 2-10	5 ¼
Workhouse	70	2411	20,500	0 6¾ 4-10	0 ¾ 2-10
Total	£31 0	5226	43,618	1s. 2 9-10	1d. ½ 4-10

TABLE OF THE NUMBER OF SICK ATTENDED BY THE PAROCHIAL MEDICAL OFFICERS IN SIX MONTHS,—Ending 31st March, 1848, and the remuneration per case, and per visit.

TABLE II.

Parish of Bethnal Green.	Salary.	Casesattended.	Visits paid.	Rate per case.	Rate per Visit.
District No. 1.	£35	508	5210	1s. 4½ 1-10	1½d. 4-10
— — 2.	35	462	3120	1 6 7-10	2½ 7-10
— — 3.	35	425	4026	1 7¾	2— 3-10
— — 4.	35	845	7258	0 9¾ 7-10	1— 6-10
— — 5.	30	204	1717	2 11¼ 1-10	4— 7-10
Workhouse.	35	1840	15640	0 4½ 2-10	½ 1-10
Total.	£205	4284	36971	0 11¼ 9-10	1¼d 3-10

TABLE 3

CASES OF DISEASE ATTENDED BY THE PAROCHIAL

Zymotic seases.	DISTRICT, No. 1.					DISTRICT, No. 2.					DISTRICT, No. 3.				
	1846 4th Qua.	1847 1st Qua.	1847 2nd Qua.	1847 3rd Qua.	Total.	1846 4th Qua.	1847 1st Qua.	1847 2nd Qua.	1847 3rd Qua.	Total.	1846 4th Qua.	1847 1st Qua.	1847 2nd Qua.	1847 3rd Qua.	Total.
Smallpox	.	.	2	7	9	.	1	3	12	16	1	5	6	10	22
Measles	4	6	6	1	17	.	.	9	4	13	2	1	1	7	11
Scarlatina	.	.	.	.	.	4	.	3	9	16	.	1	3	10	14
Hooping Cough	4	2	.	3	9	.	.	.	2	2	2	.	.	.	2
Croup	.	.	.	.	.	.	.	.	.	.	.	.	.	.	.
Thrush	.	.	1	.	1	.	1	.	.	1	.	.	.	.	.
Diarrhœa	4	7	7	24	42	6	8	7	20	41	5	2	9	24	40
Dysentery	.	.	.	.	.	.	1	1	.	2	.	.	.	.	.
Cholera	.	.	.	.	.	.	.	.	.	.	.	.	.	.	.
Influenza	.	.	.	.	.	.	.	.	.	.	.	.	.	.	.
Ague	.	.	.	.	.	.	.	6	.	6	.	.	.	.	.
Remittent Fever	.	.	1	.	1	1	.	.	.	1	.	.	.	.	.
Typhus	25	23	20	52	120	14	10	21	40	85	21	13	11	33	78
Erysipelas	.	2	.	.	2	1	8	2	2	11	1	1	1	2	4
Total	37	40	37	87	201	26	29	50	89	194	32	22	31	86	171
Total Cases attended	101	135	104	175	515	98	126	143	169	536	132	113	98	156	499
Relative Proportion of Zymotic to other Diseases	36·6	29·6	35·5	49·7	39·0	28·3	23·0	35·0	52·7	36·1	24·2	19·4	31·6	53·8	34·4
Deaths from Zymotic Diseases	2	.	3	6	11	2	7	7	11	27	1	2	3	9	15

INFLUENZA—There are no returns of cases of this disease except, in District No. 4, and in the workhouse; this is attributed chiefly to the disease passing into the stage of Bronchitis before it is seen by the medical officer; the same explanation applies to district No. 2. In district No. 3, the disease is said to have passed into common fever, and in No. 5, the healthy district, a considerable number of cases of catarrh are marked, some of which may probably have been cases of influenza.

REMITTENT FEVER—I am unable to account for cases of Remittent Fever occurring only in district No. 4.

TYPHUS—Nearly all diseases, it mattered not of what kind, assumed the typhoid form, and many merged into typhus. This was more peculiarly the case in the densely populated and filthy districts, Nos. 3 and 4.

TABLE 3.

MEDICAL OFFICERS, FROM Oct. 1st, 1846, TILL Oct 1st 1847.

DISTRICT, No. 4.					DISTRICT, No. 5.					WORKHOUSE.					Sum Total.	Proportion of Zymotics to each other.	Mortality.	Mortality per Cent.
1846 4th Qua.	1847 1st Qua.	1847 2nd Qua.	1847 3rd Qua.	Total.	1846 4th Qua.	1847 1st Qua.	1847 2nd Qua.	1847 3rd Qua.	Total.	1846 4th Qua.	1847 1st Qua.	1847 2nd Qua.	1847 3rd Qua.	Total.				
	6	10	3	9			1	3	4	1	3	18	10	32	92	5·77	15	16·3
	1	10	15	25	2	2			4		2	58	60	130	8·11	20	15·3
2	7	7	3	6		3	7		10	7	8		16	31	77	4·64	19	23·3
3	1	7	2	19	1	5		1	7		10	3	8	21	60	3·76	13	21·6
1				1											1	·06	1	100
	2	2	4	9											11	·67	2	18·1
19	8	17	100	144	1	3	1	7	12	44	35	47	155	281	560	35·01	28	5·0
1	3	2	3	9											11	·67	1	9·0
			4	4											4	·25		
4	5	1	1	11							7	1		8	19	1·19		
		2	2											8	·56		
2	3	3	7	15											17	1·06		
18	9	15	96	138	7	6	3	7	23	11	17	10	50	88	532	33·45	18	3·3
8	9	2	11	30	1	3	1	1	6	4	2	1	8	15	68	4·27	3	4·5
58	54	59	251	422	12	22	12	19	66	67	82	82	305	536	1590		119	7·48
205	246	215	330	996	67	70	68	64	269	422	522	582	885	2411	5226			
28·3	21·9	2·4	76·0	4·3	18·0	31·4	19·1	29·7	24·5	15·8	15·7	14·0	34·3	22·2	30·4			
5	4	5	13	27	1	2	2	1	6	3	6	2	27	38			119	

CROUP.—One case of Croup or Cynanche-trachealis occurred in District No. 1, but of a strictly inflammatory character.

Two cases occurred in district No. 5, the one preceding Measles, the other accompanying Scarlatina, the latter died; these are marked under Measles and Scarlatina. One also occurred in the workhouse of an inflammatory character.

THRUSH—This disease was common among the infants in the workhouse, and was managed by the sick nurses, and is not returned in this table.

CHOLERA—No decided cases of Cholera have occurred, except in the dirty District No.4; many severe cases of bilious sickness have, however, taken place during the warm weather.

An examination of the succeeding table proves that, while the whole amount of cases deriving medical relief under the Poor Law, in the healthy district No. 5, amounted to only 269; in the unhealthy district, No. 4, characterised by the grossest foulness, the cases amounted to 996;—while zymotic diseases prostrated 24·5 per cent. of the sick in the healthy district, they attacked 42·3 per cent. of the sick in the unhealthy district;—while 23 persons were attacked with fever, and 12 with diarrhœa, in the healthy district, 138 were attacked with fever, and 144 with diarrhœa, in the unhealthy district.

The expense to the public, for the relief of sickness, should be for that proportion which is unavoidable, and which is inherent to the natural condition of man. All other expence, for avoidable sickness, is a tax paid by the public for their neglect of the health and lives of their fellow men:—Yet, more than 30 per cent. of the cases of sickness, attended by the Poor Law Medical Officers, in Bethnal-green, arises from epidemic diseases, the greater, by far the greater, part of this sickness is unnecessary and preventible. The expence, such as it is, is unnecessary, the labour of the medical officers is unnecessary, and their free and liberal exposure to typhus, is, in a great measure, unnecessary;—because all could be avoided.

1590 cases of epidemic, or zymotic diseases, proved to be, to a great extent, preventible diseases, sought parochial medical relief; 5226 cases of disease received medical relief at the hands of parish, in the year ending Oct. 1, 1847.

This relief was distributed by five medical officers, at an expense of £310 to the parish. This remuneration returned to the gentlemen engaged, a clear sum of 1s. 2d. and 2-10 for the trouble of visiting and providing each case with medicine, but, this munificent and liberal conduct of the wise and beneficent guardians of the poor, does not appear in so good a light, when it is considered, that each case was visited many times, and, that if the number of visits to the poor sick, be calculated, it is found that the aggregate amounts to a sum of 43·618. The remuneration, if divided by this sum, presents to each of the medical gentlemen (on an average) the sum of 1½d. 4-10 for his visit, out of which must be deducted the cost of the medicine to be supplied.

Alas! Are not such statements sufficient to prove the absolute mockery, the complete falseness, the utter worthlessness in the working, of the present system of medical relief to the poor. Do they not prove the severity of the labour entailed on the oppressed surgeon, while they exhibit the *most considerate* regard for the poor.

TABLE IV.

The following Table illustrates the amount of mortality and the number of births in the different quarters of the year specified, and in the different districts of the parish:—

TABLE OF BIRTHS AND DEATHS IN THE DISTRICTS OF THE PARISH OF BETHNAL GREEN IN 12 MONTHS, ENDING Oct. 1, 1847.

(Compiled from the returns of the Registrar-general.)

MALES.	GREEN Dist. 1846 4th Qr.	1847 1st Qr.	1847 2nd Qr.	1847 3rd Qr.	CHURCH Dist. 1846 4th Qr.	1847 1st Qr.	1847 2nd Qr.	1847 3rd Qr.	TOWN Dist. 1846 4th Qr.	1847 1st Qr.	1847 2nd Qr.	1847 3rd Qr.	HACKNEY-Rd Dist. 1846 4th Qr.	1847 1st Qr.	1847 2d Qr.	1847 3rd Qr.
Number of Deaths.	82	77	78	98	54	49	50	43	70	60	58	81	44	66	42	54
Number of Births.	89	94	82	78	96	86	96	81	93	117	110	111	81	116	92	106
FEMALES.																
Number of Deaths.	77	76	68	104	50	56	30	52	83	56	34	71	49	76	60	52
Number of Births.	86	90	98	75	84	89	87	74	107	103	80	84	99	108	111	87
Total Deaths.	159	153	146	202	104	105	80	95	153	116	92	152	93	142	102	106
Total Births.	175	184	180	153	180	175	183	155	200	220	190	195	180	224	203	193

Total Deaths, Male and Female . . . 2000. | Total Births, Male and Female . . . 2990.

The following Table shows the proportion of deaths and births in the different districts, and in the whole parish:—

TABLE V.

TABLE OF DEATHS AND BIRTHS IN THE PARISH OF BETHNAL GREEN IN 12 MONTHS, ENDING Oct. 1, 1847.

(Extracted and compiled from the returns to the Registrar-general.)

DISTRICTS.		Males.	Females.	Total
Green	Deaths	335	325	660*
	Births.	343	349	692†
Church	Deaths	196	188	384
	Births.	359	334	693
Town	Deaths	269	244	513
	Births.	431	374	805
Hackney-road	Deaths	206	237	443
	Births.	395	405	800
Sum Total of	Deaths	1006	994	2000
	Births,	1528	1462	2990

* This number includes 39 deaths from Zymotic diseases, and 130 deaths from other causes in the Workhouse. Also two deaths from Zymotic diseases, and eighty-eight deaths from other causes in the Lunatic Asylum, in all 259 deaths, which should be substracted from 660, leaving 301 to represent the true mortality in the district.

† This number includes 39 births in the Workhouse which should be substracted from 692 leaving 553 to represent the number of births in the district.

The succeeding Table points out the deaths from zymotic diseases in the periods and districts specified:—

TABLE VI.

DEATHS FROM ZYMOTIC DISEASES IN THE DISTRICTS OF THE PARISH OF BETHNAL-GREEN IN ONE YEAR, ENDING Oct. 1, 1847. FOUR REFERS TO THE FOURTH QUARTER OF 1846 ONE, TWO, THREE TO THE FIRST, SECOND AND THIRD QUARTERS OF 1847.

(Compiled from the returns to the Registrar-general.).

Districts.	Church.				Town.				Hackney-rd				Green.				Deaths.
Diseases.	4	1	2	3	4	1	2	3	4	1	2	3	4	1	2	3	Total.
Small-pox	..	..	1	5	2	6	4	13	..	1	..	4	..	..	1	5	42
Measles	..	..	2	5	4	3	4	9	1	3	4	4	2	1	2	18	62
Scarlatina	4	1	3	7	17	1	1	6	6	3	4	1	3	1	8	13	79
Hooping-cough	..	..	2	1	15	1	4	2	5	8	6	4	6	12	7	4	77
Croup	1	1	1	..	4	11		1	2	2	1	2	..	2	1	1	30
Thrush	..	3	..	..	1	..			1	..	2	1	..	..		1	9
Diarrhœa	3	2	2	15	3	..	5	27	4	2	..	12	4	5	5	29	118
Dysentery	..	..	..	1	..	..	..		1	..	1	..	1	1	1	3	9
Cholera	..	..	..	..	..	..	..	3	..	..	..	1	..	..	..	2	6
Influenza	..	..	..	..	..	..	..	1	1	..	..	..	2	..	..	1	5
Ague	..	..	..	..	..	..	..		..	..	..	..	..	..	..	..	
Remit.-fever	..	..	..	..	..	..	..		..	..	..	1	..	..	..	1	1
Typhus	2	1	4	5	2	1	2	8	4	8	3	5	4	1	12	9	74
Erysipelas	..	..	1	1	..	..	1	1	1	..	1	1	..	..	1	1	9
Total Deaths	11	8	16	39	48	22	21	71	26	27	22	39	22	23	38	88	521
Sum Total	74				162				114				171				
Proportion of Deaths to the Population.	1 in 260				1 in 137				1 in 195				1 in 109				1 in 158.

The following table presents a summary of the preceding table, and has reference to the whole parish:—

TABLE VII.

PROPORTION OF DEATHS, FROM ALL CAUSES, AND FROM ZY-MOTIC DISEASES, AND OF BIRTHS TO THE POPULATION IN THE PARISH OF BETHNAL GREEN IN 12 MONTHS, ENDING OCT. 1. 1847.

(Compiled from the returns to the Registrar-general.)

DISTRICTS.	Estimated population corrected for increase up to June 10 1847	Proportion of Deaths from all causes to the population.			Proportion of Deaths from Zymotic dis. to the popn.	Proportion of Births to the population.
		Males.	Females	Total		
Green.. ..	18·654	1 in 55	1 in 57	1 in 28	1 in 109	1 in 26·9
* Corrected	*17·228		†1 in 57	‡1 in 132		‖1 in 31·1
Church ..	19·240	1 in 98	1 in 102	1 in 50	1 in 260	1 in 27·7
Town.. ..	22·250	1 in 82	1 in 91	1 in 43	1 in 137	1 in 27·6
Hackney-road	22·286	1 in 108	1 in 92	1 in 50	1 in 195	1 in 27·8
Total	82·430	1 in 81	1 in 82	1 in 41	1 in 158	1 in 27·5

* The Workhouse and Lunatic Asylum are sources of error. The population of this district requires to be corrected by the substraction of the average number contained, during the 12 months, in the Workhouse, 796, and in the Lunatic Asylum 630, in all 1,426. The true population of the district is then represented by 17,228.

† The number of deaths in the Workhouse, 169; and in the Lunatic Asylum, 90; requires to be substracted from the number of deaths. The proportion would then be as above.

‡ The number of deaths in the Workhouse from zymotic causes, 39; and in the Lunatic Asylum two, requires to be substracted. The proportion is then changed to the above number.

‖ The number of births in the Workhouse, 39; requires to be substracted. When the proportion is left as above.

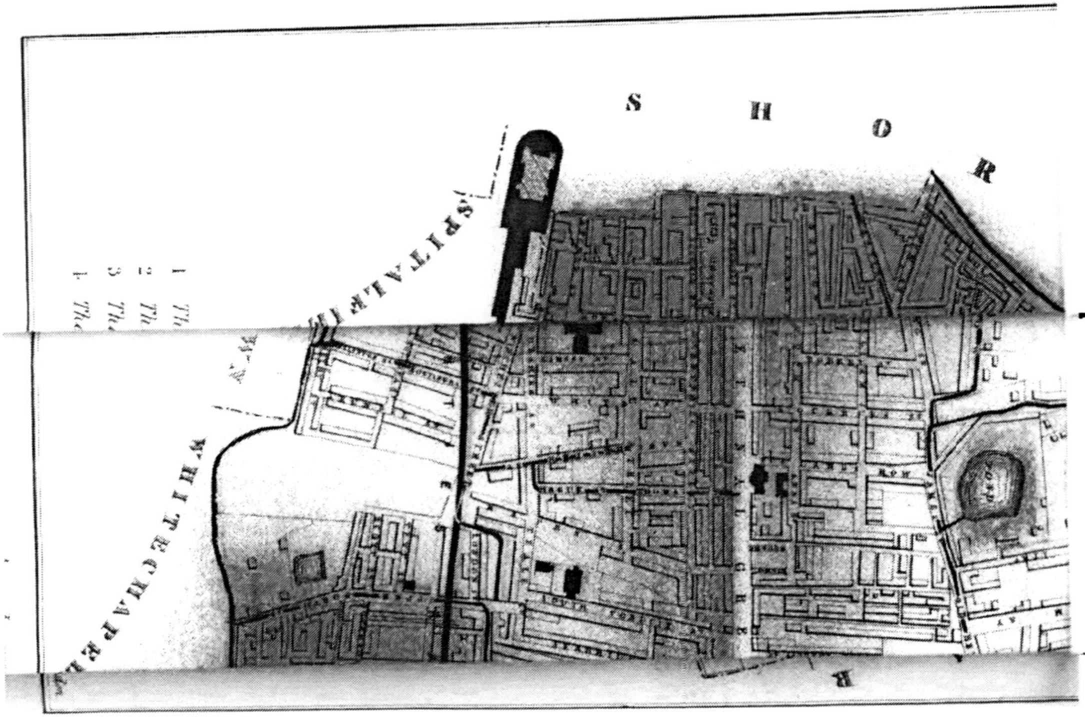
S H O R
SPITALFI
WHITECHAPEL

The relative healthiness of the different districts therefore is as follows :—The Green, the Church, Hackney Road, the Town. The relative mortality being 1 in 57, 50, 50, and 43. The relative proportion of deaths from Zymotic diseases, 1 in 132, 260, 195, and in 137. The relative proportion of births is 1 in 31·1., 27·7., 27·8., 27·6.

It is readily understood by the accounts contained in the preceding pages, why there should be so great a difference in the mortality in the Green, and in the Town districts. The one open and free, the other close and confined. But the great proportion in which it suffers from epidemic diseases could scarcely have been anticipated, but must be traced to the abominable filthiness, and the great amount of vegetable and animal remains surrounding the houses of the poor, as well as to its exposure to the emanations from the marshes which surround it, and against which it has no defence, but itself acts as the barrier to their spread towards London. The facts, however, most clearly point out that in a poor population, surrounded by much filth, with scarcely any drainage and still less sewerage, with street cleansing greatly neglected, and a high mortality from epidemics; a very low rate of mortality can be obtained by the avoidance of over crowding and an abundant supply of air. And that the causes which destroy the poor, arising from filth and the absence of facilities for its removal, are not only epidemic diseases, but the excess in several, and the greater frequency of all those other diseases to which man is subject.

The law by which an all wise Providence supplies the loss caused by an excessive mortality is clearly enough demonstrated here; for, while in the comparatively healthy district the ratio of deaths is 1 in 57, and the ratio of births 1 in 31·1., in the unhealthy district the ratio of deaths is 1 in 43, and the ratio of births 1 in 27·6.

The accompanying lithographic plate of the parish exhibits the Disease Mist which overhangs it, and destroys, and enfeebles, the population; this Angel of death not only breathes pestilence, and causes an afflicted people to render back dust to dust, but is accompanied with that destroying Angel which breathes a moral pestilence; for where the seeds of physical death are thickly sown, and yield an abundant harvest, there moral death overshadows the land,—and sweeps with the besom of destruction to an eternal gulf.

TABLE VIII.

The following Table exhibits the number of males and females that have died in one year, and the ages at which they have died; and also the number living at the termination of a given period:—

THE STREAM OF LIFE, OR TABLE OF MORTALITY IN THE PARISH OF BETHNAL-GREEN IN TWELVE MONTHS, ENDING OCT. 1, 1847.

(Extracted and compiled from the returns to the Register-general.

Age.	Males.	Females.	Total.	Of 2,000 there are living at the termination of each year.	Age.	Males.	Females.	Total.	Of 2,000 there are living at the termination of each year.
1	310	354	664	1336	53	5	9	14	493
2	83	56	139	1197	54	14	3	17	476
3	38	36	74	1123	55	5	7	12	464
4	16	33	49	1074	56	9	5	14	450
5	18	15	33	1041	57	13	9	22	428
6	12	5	17	1024	58	5	9	14	414
7	9	11	20	1004	59	7	5	12	402
8	6	6	12	992	60	17	8	25	377
9	9	6	15	977	61	6	9	15	362
10	5	3	8	969	62	11	10	21	341
11	6	4	10	959	63	8	5	13	328
12	7	2	9	950	64	6	9	15	313
13	3	4	7	943	65	9	9	18	295
14	2	1	3	940	66	7	10	17	278
15	2	3	5	935	67	9	5	14	264
16	1	4	5	930	68	7	2	9	255
17	5	4	9	921	69	5	9	14	241
18	2	5	7	914	70	10	10	20	221
19	4	4	8	906	71	6	4	10	211
20	4	7	11	895	72	5	11	16	195
21	4	9	13	882	73	11	2	13	182
22	4	3	7	875	74	8	11	19	163
23	2	4	6	869	75	9	7	16	147
24	3	6	9	860	76	10	4	14	133
25	4	4	8	852	77	13	8	21	112
26	5	6	11	841	78	10	10	20	92
27	2	5	7	834	79	6	2	8	84
28	10	9	19	815	80	8	6	14	70
29	5	6	11	804	81	4	7	11	59
30	12	11	23	781	82	4	5	9	50
31	7	4	11	770	83	4	6	10	40
32	5	5	10	760	84	4	4	8	32
33	6	7	13	747	85	2		2	30
34	3	6	9	738	86	4	1	5	25
35	4	8	12	726	87	2	2	4	21
36	10	7	17	709	88	1	3	4	17
37	6	8	14	695	89	1	1	2	15
38	4	6	10	685	90	1	1	2	13
39	7	5	12	673	91	2	1	3	10
40	9	10	19	654	92	1	1	2	8
41	6	7	13	641	93	1	1	2	6
42	7	4	11	630	94	1		1	5
43	5	6	11	619	95	1	1	2	3
44	9	2	11	608	96				
45	9	14	23	585	97				
46	10	2	12	573	98				
47	9	1	10	563	99	1		1	2
48	6	5	11	552	100				
49	6	11	17	535	101	1		1	1
50	5	8	13	522	102				
51	4	4	8	514	103		1	1	0
52		5	7	507					

Total Males, 1006. Females, 994 = 200.

From this Table it follows that of 2,000 deaths—

664 occurred under 1 year of age, or	. . .	33·1 per cent.
803 occurred under 2 years of age, or	. . .	40·1 ,,
959 occurred under 5 years of age, or	. . .	47·9 ,,
1,065 occurred under 15 years of age, or	. . .	53·2 ,,
1,528 occurred under 60 years of age, or	. . .	79·9 ,,

And that the average age of death was—

Of males		25·2 ,,
Of females		26·8 ,,
Of males above 1 year		41·1 ,,
Of females "		37·3½ ,,
Of males and females, of all ages, . . .		26·6 ,,

It follows that the average age at death has increased by 10 months for every individual during the last 8 years, having been 25 years and 8 months in 1839, but 26 years 6 months in 1847.

It is likewise proved by the foregoing tables that the relative mortality has not diminished, but rather increased; for while the mortality in 1832 was 1 in 41, and in 1841 1 in 43, it is now, again, 1 in 41. The proportion of births, by the extraordinary law which prevails, has increased, notwithstanding the high mortality; for while the proportion in 1841 was to the population as 1 in 28, the proportion now is 1 in 27·5.

The following Table illustrates the mortality from epidemic diseases:

TABLE IX.

TABLE OF MORTALITY FROM EPIDEMIC OR ZYMOTIC DISEASES, IN THE PARISH OF BETHNAL-GREEN, IN 12 MONTHS, ENDING OCT. 1, 1847.

(Compiled and extracted from the returns of the Registrar-general.)

Age	Males.	Females.	Total.	Stream of death from Epidemics	Age.	Males.	Females.	Total.	Stream of death from Epidemics	Age.	Males.	Females.	Total.	Stream of death from Epidemics
ms. 6	43	35	78	523	30	..	2	2	62	60	..	1	1	25
yrs. 1	66	62	128	445	31	3	..	3	60	61	1	..	1	24
2	44	37	81	317	32	1	2	3	57	62	..	1	1	23
3	19	21	40	236	33	1	..	1	54	63	1	..	1	22
4	9	26	35	196	34	..	..	..	..	64	1	..	1	21
5	11	12	23	161	35	..	1	1	53	65	1	..	1	20
6	7	5	12	138	36	..	..	..	..	66	1	2	3	19
3	5	7	12	126	37	..	2	2	52	67	1	..	1	16
8	4	5	9	114	38	..	..	..	..	68	..	2	2	15
9	4	2	6	105	39	..	..	..	..	69	..	..	..	..
10	1	3	4	99	40	1	..	1	50	70	1	..	1	13
11	4	2	6	95	41	1	2	3	49	71	..	1	1	12
12	2	1	3	89	42	1	..	1	46	72	..	2	2	11
13	1	1	2	86	43	..	..	..	..	73	1	1	2	9
14	..	..	..	..	44	1	1	2	45	74	..	..	..	..
15	1	2	3	84	45	2	1	3	43	75	..	..	..	..
16	..	..	..	..	46	2	..	2	40	76	..	..	..	..
17	1	..	1	81	47	1	..	1	38	77	1	2	3	7
18	1	2	3	80	48	1	..	1	37	78	..	..	..	..
19	1	4	5	77	49	1	3	4	36	79	..	..	..	..
20	2	1	3	72	50	1	..	1	32	80	..	..	..	..
21	..	3	3	69	51	1	..	1	31	81	..	..	..	..
22	..	..	..	..	52	..	..	..	..	82	1	1	2	4
23	..	..	..	..	53	..	..	..	..	83	..	..	..	..
24	1	..	1	66	54	..	1	1	30	84	1	..	1	2
25	..	..	..	..	55	1	..	1	29	85	..	..	..	..
26	2	..	2	65	56	..	..	..	..	86	..	..	..	..
27	..	..	..	..	57	..	2	2	28	87	..	..	..	..
28	1	..	1	63	58	..	..	..	..	99	..	..	..	..
29	..	..	..	..	59	1	..	1	26	89	..	1	1	1

Total deaths of males, 261; of females, 262. Total, 523.

THE STREAM OF LIFE
IN THE PARISH OF BETHNAL GRE[EN]
FORMED FROM THE REGISTER OF DEATHS IN THE YEAR

The lowest darkened line marks the deaths of Males, from
The middle darkened line, the deaths of both sexes from
The upper darkened line, the deaths from all causes.

Deaths from Zymotic diseases { Males 261. } Total, 523.   Deaths from all ca[uses]
{ Females 262. }

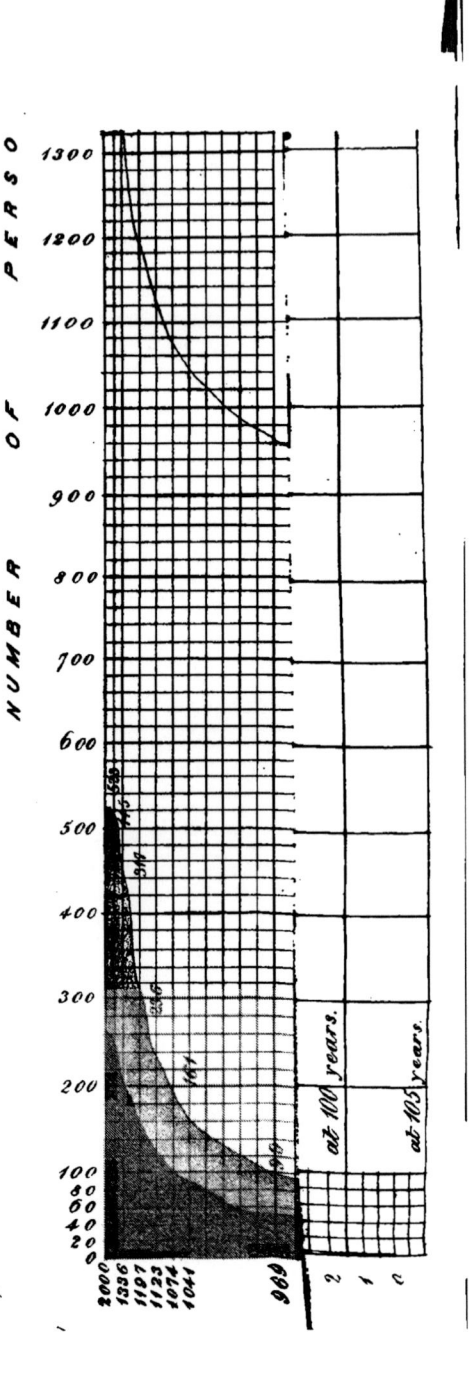

It is proved from the foregoing Tables, that of the mortality which occurs in Bethnal-Green, more than a fourth arises from epidemic diseases; of 2,000 deaths, 523 were due to epidemic diseases. Of these 523 deaths,

78 occurred under 6 months.
206 ,, during the first and before the completion of the second year of life.
287 ,, ,, ,, ,, ,, " third year of life, and
305 ,, ,, ,, before the completion of the fifth year of life.

In Table No. 6, the relative proportion of these epidemic diseases, one to the other, is shown. It is impossible, with the full knowledge that the fatality of epidemic diseases may be infinitely diminished, if the diseases themselves cannot be entirely averted, to view more than a fourth of the mortality as the result of these diseases, without arriving at the conclusion that a very large proportion of the children which are born are ushered into life but to perish of loathsome diseases. And when we consult Table No. 1, we are further taught that these diseases prevail to an alarming extent, and constitute a very great part of the most anxious toils of the medical officers who attend the poor. It is indeed appalling to consider the enormous mortality which takes place among the children of the poor. Thus, in Bethnal-green, among the children of the gentry under 10 years of age, the mortality, in 1839, was, to the total of deaths in the same class, 22·0 per cent.—Tradesmen, 55·3.—Artificers, 65·1.

During last year,

Of 664 deaths at 1 year of age, 206 deaths arose from epidemics.
139 ,, 2 years ,, 81 ,, ,,
74 ,, 3 ,, ,, 40 ,, ,,
49 ,, 4 ,, ,, 35 ,, ,,
54 ,, 5 ,, ,, 23 ,, ,,

The annexed Lithographic Table exhibits in a simple manner the rapid diminution of life which takes place, especially during infancy and childhood. It points out, as Addison has beautifully done, in his "Vision of Mirza," how thickly are set in early years the traps in the bridge of life which man has to traverse.

Addison compares "human life to a bridge consisting of three score and ten arches, with several broken arches, which, added to those which were entire, made up the number to about a hundred." I see multitudes of people passing over it," said I; "and a black cloud hanging on each end of it. As I looked more attentively, I saw several of the passengers dropping through the bridge into the great tide that flowed underneath it; and upon further examination perceived there were innumerable trap doors that lay concealed in the bridge which the passengers no sooner trod upon than they fell into the tide, and immediately disappeared. These hidden pitfalls were set very thick at the entrance of the bridge." "They grew thinner towards the middle, but multiplied and lay closer together towards the end of the arches that were entire." The table represents a stream of 2000 persons "breaking through the cloud, follows them in their passage over each arch, and paints the "hidden pitfalls," through which they disappear. Alas! how few does it represent as reaching the broken arches.

The following Tables convey the most distressing information as to the premature death of the great mass of the poor:—

TABLE X.

"In a return obtained" by Mr. Chadwick, "it appears that of 1,263 deaths in Bethnal Green amongst the labouring classes, in the year 1839, no less than 782, or 1 in 147, died at their own residences under 5 years of age. One in 15 of the deaths occurred between 5 and 10, the age when employment commences. The proportion of deaths which occurred between 10 and 15, the period at which full employment usually takes place, is 1 in 60 only."

In Bethnal Green the average age of death in the year 1839 was as follows, in the several classes.

No. of Deaths.	BETHNAL GREEN. Population 74,087.	Average Age of Deceased.
101	Gentlemen, Professional Men, and their Families.	45
273	Tradesmen, and their Families.	26
1,258	Mechanics, Servants, Labourers, and their Families.	16

Let us compare this Table with the following Tables of the average age at death in the same year, in the same classes, in the four adjoining parishes.

No. of Deaths.	HACKNEY. Population 42,274.	Average Age of Deceased.
61	Gentry, and their Families.	47
228	Tradesmen, and their Families.	29
237	Artizans, and their Families.	27

No. of Deaths.	SHOREDITCH. Population 83,552	Average Age of Deceased.
86	Gentry, and their Families.	47
303	Tradesmen, and their Families.	23
1,300	Artizans, and their Families.	19

No. of Deaths.	WHITECHAPEL. Population 71,758.	Average Age of Deceased.
21	Gentry, and their Families.	47
272	Tradesmen, and their Families.	26
1,378	Artizans, and their Families.	25

No. of Deaths.	POPLAR. Population 31,091.	Average Age of Deceased.
23	Gentry, and their Families.	43
84	Tradesmen, and their Families.	26
475	Artizans, and their Families.	25

Let us also recognise the following facts, as conveying instructive lessons regarding the sanitary state of Bethnal Green, compared with the adjoining parishes. It is compiled from the Supplement to the Report on the Sanitary Condition of the Labouring Population, and refers to the Year 1839. It exhibits the absolute waste of life in each of the parishes, the early age at which death takes place, and the relative loss of life to the tradesmen, and artizans, and to every individual in the locality:—

TABLE XI.

TABLE EXHIBITING THE PROPORTION, AND EXCESS OF DEATHS, THE AVERAGE AGE AT DEATH, AND THE LOSS OF LIFE AS COMPARED WITH A HEALTHY STANDARD.

Parishes.	Population.	Proportion of Deaths to the Population—1 in every	Excess in the positive No. of Deaths beyond the healthy Standard.	Average Age at Death.	Loss of Life. To the Gentry.	To Tradesmen.	To Artizans.	To every Individual.[*]
Bethnal Green.	74,087	41	794	22	"	yr. 15	yr. 21	yr. m 10 5
Hackney.	42,274	56	155	31	"	10	12	3 7
Shoreditch.	83,552	38	732	26	"	16	20	8 1
Whitechapel.	71,758	31	768	26	"	13	14	8 1
Poplar.	31,091	47	186	28	"	13	14	6 9

[*] In 841. Compared with Camberwell.

The following Table, referring to the year 1841, demonstrates the extravagance and waste occasioned by the present *Death and Dirt Tax*. It exhibits the relative proportions of deaths from epidemic, endemic, and contagious diseases, called Zymotic Diseases, to the population; and the money-loss entailed on the parishes by a neglect of Sanitary Measures, supposing that no greater loss occurred than takes place relatively in Camberwell.

TABLE XII.

LOSS ON THE YEAR'S DEATHS IN LIFE, &c.

	Life One in every	Money*	Sickness.	Funerals.	Labour.	Total.
Bethnal Green.	99	£31	£4,648	£830	£23,157	£28,635
Hacknney.	269	"	"	"	"	"
Shoreditch.	123	47	14,756	2,635	51,982	69,373
Whitechapel.	83	114	20,461	3,655	131,328	155,444
Poplar.	140	73	924	165	25,842	26,931

* The calculation of the Money Loss refers to the value of productive labour at 10s. per week for men, and 5s. per week for women; say 7s. 6d. per week for each adult.

In endeavouring to estimate the actual loss of life to Bethnal-green from the neglect of sanitary measures, and which is capable of prevention, I will assume that the mortality can be reduced to 2 per cent., or 1 in 50. I am quite convinced that such a reduction is not by any means the full measure of the gain, but I am unwilling to use an exaggerated standard; and as a mortality of 2 per cent. has been conceded by the calmest and most dispassionate judges, as well as by the partizans of sanitary reform, I trust that even this standard will be sufficient to arouse every prudent, selfish or benevolent, mercenary or philanthropic man, as well as Christian, to exertion. The motives cannot but be confessed to be all powerful.

Bethnal-green possessed, on an estimate, corrected for the increase of population, on the 1st of July, 1847, a population of 82,430. The increase of the population, by the influx of new inhabitants into new houses, has been fully counterbalanced by the pulling down of numerous old houses in densely populated neighbourhoods, by the Railway Company. Under the beneficial influence of sanitary regulations, a mortality of 1,648 would occur, but during the year which has been taken 2,000 deaths occurred. A preventible excess of mortality of 352, therefore, has taken place. The annual deaths of 352 persons is the price in life, paid by Bethnal-green to support its present filthy state—a costly, and extravagant, and fearful sacrifice.

It has been the custom by most sanitary statists to bring forward the average age at death, as a test of the sanitary state of a district. In accordance, therefore, with this custom, though not placing implicit dependence on it as a test, I have given a return of the average ages of males and females at, and above 1 year, and of the whole population, at death. It is to be borne in mind that the death of one person at 103 (the greatest age obtained) counts for the death of 103 infants below 1 year of age.

Bethnal-green has been exhibited as having a very low average age at death. It is too notoriously unhealthy to necessitate any questioned data to support the fact of its unhealthiness. Let us then examine whether it really has an average so much lower than other spots considered as having a higher average age at death. For instance, the average age of death was, in 1841, in

Bethnal-green	26	Marylebone	29
Clerkenwell	26	St. George's, Hanover-square.	31·3
St. Giles's and St. George's	28	Kensington	32

But if the distribution of the population, according to age, be equalized in these several districts, in accordance with the views of some critical statists, it appears that, for the amount of population, St. Giles's and St. George's, Bloomsbury, is the most unhealthy. The order would be as follows:—

St. Giles's and St. George's	24·34	Bethnal-green	25·80
Marylebone	24·52	Kensington	26·71
Clerkenwell	24·84	St. George's, Hanover-square	28·13

The rate of mortality follows precisely the same order.

It has been asserted, and to a certain extent, conceded that *the average age at death, is not a sound or correct means of estimating the sanitary state of a district*. On the same ground, it follows that the estimates which have been made of the number of years of life lost by a population are incorrect. By the aid of Mr. Neison's calculations, some approximation can be made as to the amount of error. One of the most unhealthy districts, according to the rough test referred to, is Bethnal-green, where the average age at death in 1841 was 25·80; and of the most healthy is Kensigton, where the average age for the same year was 32·39; being a difference of six years and a half in favour of Kensington. But if the prevailing rate of mortality in Kensington had been applied to the population of Bethnal-green, the average loss of life in 1841 would have been only 1 year. (Bethnal-green 25·80, Kensington 26·71.) Corrected then by the most severe tests, subjected to the closest scrutiny, viewed in the most favourable light, the calculation proves that Bethnal-green inflicted in 1841 a loss on its population of 1764 years of life, compared with that of Kensington.

A low average age at death is generally the result of two causes—an enormous sacrifice of life among a young population, or the prevalence of unhealthy influences. Both of these causes contribute to the low average age at death in Bethnal-green.

It is worthy of observation that the proportion of births to the population in Bethnal-green, is in accordance with the law which regulates the excess of births by the excess of mortality.

I am fully aware that the average ages at death of the gentry, tradesmen, and artizans, displayed in the latter tables, are open to some objections, and require some modifications. The objections are, Firstly, the exclusion of paupers in workhouses from the classes of tradesmen and artizans. If this class were distributed in the proportion of 1-10 to the tradesman, and 9-10 to the artizans, the average ages at death of these two classes would be raised: these averages would much more closely approximate to that of the gentry, if we took the average age at death, of all dying above 21. Secondly, that the distribution of the ages of the living has been omitted in the calculation.

I can see no necessity for comparing the longevity of the class of gentry with that of artizans (and still less for setting up the standard of health obtained by the gentry as that to be desired for the labouring classes), for the purpose of procuring sympathy with their condition, and support to the sanitary measures desired to improve that condition.

There are causes of mortality which are peculiar to each class of society, and which are common to all classes; certain of those causes which are common to all, but which peculiarly bear hard upon the poorer classes, are capable of being prevented. When, by Sanitary Improvements, these causes of disease have been averted, the solution of the problem will arise whether the occupations of the poor, (and I consider that under Sanitary Improvements, the conducting of trades and manufactures injurious to health will be included, so that their danger to health may be averted or diminished,) are more detrimental to health and life than the occupations of the middle and upper classes. At present, there can be no question, that the poorer classes are peculiarly exposed to the influences of certain proximate and exciting causes of death.

One evidence of the unhealthiness of Bethnal Green is to be found in the fact that of a Total of 2,000 deaths. 211 only occurred at 70 and upwards.

TABLE XIII.

TABLE ILLUSTRATING DEATHS AT 70 AND UPWARDS.

	Total Deaths 1839—40.	Deaths at 70, and upwards	Deaths at 70 to every 1,000.
Country	52,204	10,508	202
England and Wales	.. ..	.. ..	141
Towns	71,554	6,457	90
Bethnal Green	2,000	211	105

This return is for the 12 months ending October 1st, 1847. And another evidence is to be found in the fact, that of 1000 boys under 5 years of age there died in 1841 in

Surrey 48
Sussex 50
London 93
Bethnal Green 90

The exact numbers in Bethnal-green are Males, 9·028; Females, 8·102; calculated from the deaths in the seven years 1838-44; the population and deaths in 1841, at the same ages, were, population—Males, 5310; Females, 5429; deaths, Males, 418; Females, 422.

As there are no Foundling Hospitals, Hospitals, or Public Institutions (except the Lunatic Asylum) in Bethnal Green. These evidences are not open to any objections.

In endeavouring to estimate the amount of unnecessary sickness endured by a population, it has been customary to employ Dr. Lyon Playfair's estimate of cases of sickness to deaths. This estimate has been cavilled at, as too high; it has been proposed to reduce it from 28 to 20 or 21. But after a careful consideration of the objections urged, I do not see just grounds to reduce it, when considering Bethnal Green; and the proportionate amount of sickness and mortality occurring in the practice of the Parochial Medical Officers, tends to confirm me in my belief, that the proportion is nearly correct. If, therefore, we multiply 352 unnecessary deaths occurring in Bethnal Green by 28, we have 9,856 cases of unnecessary sickness.

Three hundred and fifty-two deaths, and 9,856 cases of disease, with all the expense and sorrow, suffering and anguish, all the lost time and labour, are at the lowest estimate, the penalties paid by Bethnal Green for its neglect of Sanitary Measures.

That these penalties do not represent the truth, I am firmly convinced, for if the Green district neglected, and foul, with no Sanitary improvements whatever introduced—has a mortality of one in fifty-seven; and if the Church and Hackney-road districts, have a mortality of one in fifty, the standard proposed in the previous calculation. Surely it is not too much to calculate that when efficient sewerage and drainage shall have been introduced; when nuisances shall be suppressed, and the streets paved and cleansed; when the houses shall be ventilated, and supplied liberally with light and water. When grave-yards shall be abolished in towns, and the physical welfare and comforts greatly increased thereby, surely it is not too much to calculate on a mortality of one in fifty-four, as the probable result. Such a calculation presents us with the following result.

A MORTALITY OF

One in fifty-four	Produces:—	One in fifty.
474	Unnecessary Deaths	352
13,272	Preventible cases of sickness	9·856
£13,272	Expense of excess of sickness	£9,856
£66,123	Loss of productive labour	£48,220
£2,370	Extra expense of funerals	£1,766
81,765	Total	59,830

The larger sum I believe to be the correct estimate of the waste money entailed on Bethnal-green, and it agrees closely with all other calculations which represent the money loss at nearly, or quite £1 per head on the population.

It is in my opinion, a *low estimate* which places it at £30,000 annually, to the Parish of Bethnal Green, as in table 12.

But not only do we find in Bethnal Green an enormous amount of sickness One person in every 8 is undergoing the prostration of disease unnecessarily; but it is notorious, that an enormous proportion of the people are unhealthy, without vigour, or physical strength, pallid, and cachetic, stunted in their growth, and of feeble organization, and prone to suffer severely from extraordinary causes of mortality. This has been well exemplified by the effects of the late epidemic, Influenza. The proportion of individuals dying of influenza, in Bethnal Green, in the second week of its prevalence, ending December 4th, was to the population as 1 in 597?, whilst in Hackney, where the same physical causes of disease do not prevail, the proportion was 1 in 1142, and in Poplar, 1 in 864; whereas in Shoreditch and Whitechapel, both of which districts resemble Bethnal Green, the mortality was respectively 1 in 751, and 1 in 535. In Lewisham and Wandsworth, the healthiest districts in the Metropolitan returns, the proportion was 1 in 3835, and 1 in 2,097. The very police are aware of the feeble physical powers of a Bethnal Green mob. Unhealthy parents beget unhealthy children, and thus premature deaths, and inability to labour, become perpetual misfortunes. Thus the stream of death flows on, feeding the sources which gave it birth.

It is necessary to advert to two apologies which may be made for a high mortality,—intemperance, and want of food. It is proved, that allowing intemperance to be a cause of high mortality, it is insufficient to explain the mortality in towns, and that the diet-roll of towns is more liberal than the country which has a lesser mortality.

The moral bearings of the question are too vast to enter upon. "Consider the lilies of the field, how they grow;" and, in the words of an estimable Sanitary Reformer, the Rev. C. Girdlestone, " Can you doubt that much more would God have man, the noblest of his creatures here below, fed, clothed, and lodged in comfort, to his own satisfaction, and to the glory of his Maker."

I have now placed before my readers a considerable mass of facts, which prove, seriatim, the enormous extent of wretchedness endured by the Community, but chiefly by the poor, from the want of efficient Sanitary Regulations, from the want, in fact, of the application to the artificial, (it can scarcely be termed civilized) state of life, in which we exist, of certain simple, plain, and apparently obvious principles. For what can be more simple, or obvious than that man's real wants are few, and abundantly provided for by a Beneficent God. Firstly Air. Secondly, Water. Thirdly, Food. Fourthly, Protection from Changes of Temperature, and the Inclemencies of the Season, by Houses, Clothing, and Fuel.

The AIR we defile in a thousand ways. The LIGHT which passes through it we reject, and deny to ourselves by our manner of building, and by heavy and oppressive taxation. WATER, we surrender up to Company Monopolists, and render scarce, and dear. FOOD has just been released from an interdict. HOUSES are ill-constructed, and adapted for human habitations, and badly arranged. CLOTHING alone is comparatively liberally supplied. While FUEL is high-priced, and a blessing little known to the poor. These are the physical wants of man;—these his necessities;—these the objects at which we must aim Firstly, to raise his physical organisation to a standard of health;—secondly, to graft on a healthy organization the highest enjoyments of existence, namely, an enlightened intellect, and sound religion. The friends of Sanitary Reform have applied themselves to the first object, and look with anxiety to the rich and powerful to aid them in their efforts, and to the poor, to acknowledge, and avail themselves of their labours.

CONCLUSION.

The conclusion at which we must necessarily arrive, when he preceding facts have been duly weighed, is, that if the inhabitants of Bethnal-green must wait till those Sanitary improvements which are so urgently required for their physical and moral welfare, shall be executed by their own authorities; centuries, and even ages may pass away with but little change from the present state of things. As far, at least, as a comprehension of the means already clearly enough demonstrated, which are necessary to, and capable of, improving the Sanitary condition of a town, this parish is steeped in the deepest ignorance. The authorities are not only utterly incapable of designing, superintending, or executing great public works, but they cannot be led to conceive their necessity. No loud demand has ever been made by them for increased sewerage, or appeal to their constituents for support to obtain it. No works of drainage, whether in connexion with the sewers which already exist, or to improve the present miserable condition of house and street drainage, have been executed by them. No supplies of water have been sought to cleanse their drains, or streets; no means but of the most imperfect, character have been adopted to remove refuse from the streets; and the contracts to remove refuse from the houses, whether of rich or poor, but especially from the houses of the poor, have been scandalously neglected; and the short-coming of the contractors most unaccountably glossed over. No knowledge of the economical results which arise from the effectual cleansing of the parish, and the sale of the accruing refuse has ever been exhibited. No investigation has ever been made into the condition of the parish, so that the facts with regard to sewage, paving, drainage, &c., should be properly known, even to the authorities themselves. The very map of the parish, by which its boundaries are ascertained, is, (or was a month ago), so tattered, old, and worn, as to be nearly falling to pieces. No attempts have ever been made to establish baths, or washhouses, to erect model lodging houses, or to contribute in any way to the improvement of the condition of the poor. No attempts have ever been made, except the talk of one, to remove or suppress the numerous horrid nuisances which abound. And Lord Morpeth's Act, cap. 9. 10. Vic., for the suppression of nuisances, has been to the authorities itself a very nuisance, in as far as it has permitted them to be responsible to the parishioners for an outrageous and most discreditable indifference as to their comfort and welfare.

The dwellings of the poor, the courts, closes, alleys, gardens, exhibit now the same condition they did many years ago, and the same degrading, demoralizing scenes of filth meet the eye, and the same sad results of early death, and feeble physical and mental organization are everywhere as apparent at the present tim as when first observed and pointed out a long time ago.

It is presumed that the most solid reason for the wretched condition of the great majority of the houses of the poor, and for the total absence of any attempts at improvement, consists in the fact that the Commissioners and guardians are themselves the chief proprietors of the dwellings of the poor, and that as they, in general pay the rates themselves, and have already exacted for their tenements the highest attainable rents any, even the slightest increase, of rates would only be an increase of their own expenditure. Under such circumstance, with the narrow and limited views entertained by such parties, to expect permanent and effectual improvements at the most limited present expenditure appears perfectly fallacious.

I hold it to be established from the foregoing observations :—

Firstly.—That an enormous amount of physical distress and of demoralisation and waste of life takes place from the existence of the present state of things.

Secondly.—That the Reports of Sanitary Commissions, and the publications of the Health of Towns and other associations have proved such sacrifices to be unnecessary and avertible.

Thirdly.—That no hope can possibly be entertained of the necessary charges being effected by the local authorities.

Fourthly.—That the knowledge of the most economical and effectual means of carrying out the necessary works, must be provided for the local authorities, and that the manner of executing them, must be supervised, by a central power; so as to prevent a wasteful expenditure of the money of the parishioners in works, irregular, imperfect, and inefficient, without any comprehensive plan or unity of design.

LIST OF CONTENTS.

Map of the parish of Bethnal-green, showing the Sewerage   Frontispiece.

	PAGE.
Map of the Medico-parochial and Registration Districts	101
Description, and Districts of the Parish	3
Rambles, one and two, District No. 1	6
Table illustrating Sanitary State of District No. 1	14
Rambles three, four and five, District No. 2	17
Table illustrating condition of Collingwood-street	22
———————Jubilee-place	26
——————Sanitary State of District No 2	31
Rambles six and seven, District No. 3	34
Table illustrating Sanitary condition of District No. 3	40
Rambles eight, nine and ten, District No. 4	42
Table illustrating Sanitary state of District No. 4	53
Rambles eleven and twelve, District No. 5	56
Table illustrating condition of Nelson-place	60
———————Sanitary state of District No. 5	63
Summary	65
Location and Structure of Dwelling-houses	66
Space alotted to Dwelling Houses	67
House accommodation	68
Lodging Houses	69
Illustration of Field-lane Lodging House	69
Warming and Ventilation	69
Ventiltaion of Public Buildings	70
Ventilation and state of St. Matthews, and St. James-the-Less, schools	72
House cleansing by Drainage	75
Table illustrating the extension of Sewage and number of communicating Drains	76
House cleansing by Removal of Refuse	77

	Page.
Privies and Cesspools	79
Paving	81
Street Cleansing	82
Sewerage	84
Map of the Sewers	see frontispiece.
Interments	85
Table represenring state of the Grave-yards	86
Nuisances	87
Water Supply	88
Sickness and Disease and Mortality	92
Tables 1 and 2 Cases of Disease attended by Parochial Medical Officers, and Remuneration	93
Table 3, Cases of Disease attended by Parochial Medical Officers	94
——— 4, Births and Deaths in Districts and Parish in Four Quarters	97
——— 5, Births and Deaths in one year	98
——— 6, Deaths from Zymotic Diseases in four Quarters and proportion to the population	99
Table 7, Proportion of Deaths from all causes, and from Zymotic Diseases, and of Births to the population in one year. Corrected for increase of population	100
Plate illustrating the Disease Mist of Bethnal-green	101
Table 8, The Stream of Life, or Table of Mortality showing the Ages at Death of all who have died	101
Table 9, Mortality from Epidemic or Zymotic Diseases, showing the ages of all who have died from these causes	104
Plate illustrating Stream of Death or Table of Mortality	105
Table 10, the average age at Death of the Gentry, Tradesmen and Artizans, in the parishes of Bethnal-green, Hackney, Shoreditch, Whitechapel and Poplar	106
Table 11, the proportion, and excess of Deaths, the average age at Death and the loss of Life as compared with a healthy standard in the same Parishes	107

	PAGE.
Table 12, Loss on the years Deaths in Life, Money, &c., to the same parishes	108
Programme of the means of ascertaining the Loss of Life	109
Table 13, Deaths at 70 and upwards in the County in England, Towns, and Bethnal-green	111
Conclusion	114

BY THE SAME AUTHOR,

Just published, 8vo., 9s. cloth,

ON FEIGNED AND FACTITIOUS DISEASES,

CHIEFLY OF SOLDIERS AND SEAMEN,

ON THE MEANS USED TO SIMULATE OR PRODUCE THEM,

and on

THE BEST MODES OF DISCOVERING IMPOSTORS.

Containing

A FULL EXPOSITION OF THE

MEANS OF DISTINGUISHING BETWEEN

THE FEIGNED AND THE REAL MANIAC, AND THE
MORAL MANIAC AND THE CRIMINAL.

Also, Price 1s.,

A LECTURE

ON THE

UNHEALTHINESS OF LONDON,

AND THE

NECESSITY OF REMEDIAL MEASURES.

LONDON: JOHN CHURCHILL.

"It contains, in very clear and concise language, a full statement of the case for the 'Health of Towns' party."—*Medical Gazette.*

"It is full of statistics and valuable opinions, and embraces almost the whole of the Sanitary question."—*Health of Towns Magazine.*

"A Lecture eminently calculated to advance the intentions of the new (Health of London) Association."—*Evening Sun.*